DATE DUE

OCT 7 1969			
OCT 1 2 1970			
GAYLORD			PRINTED IN U.S.A.

CROSSCURRENTS *Modern Critiques*

CROSSCURRENTS *Modern Critiques*

Harry T. Moore, *General Editor*

John Henry Raleigh

Time, Place, and Idea

ESSAYS ON THE NOVEL

WITH A PREFACE BY
Harry T. Moore

Carbondale and Edwardsville

SOUTHERN ILLINOIS UNIVERSITY PRESS

FEFFER & SIMONS, INC.

London and Amsterdam

PREFACE

IN THESE ESSAYS John Henry Raleigh considers a number of novels—American, German, English—of the last two centuries. He writes with a sense of history which gives a special value to his critical insights, and he is always conscious, as he tells us, of the principle of polarity as it operates in fiction. He has written a book on the modern novel that is both challenging and highly satisfying.

In his scrutiny of specific novels and in his study of the change in the novel itself over the past two centuries, Mr. Raleigh shows how the medium became transformed, and how, as it went more and more inward, it brought about an alteration in our view of history. One of Mr. Raleigh's essays deals specifically with our reaction, in the novel as in life, away from Victorian morality.

Even when dealing with a single novel, Mr. Raleigh calls up important social facts. His discussion of F. Scott Fitzgerald's The Great Gatsby, for example, treats more than the technical and thematic aspects of the story; it shows how the book is "about American history as a whole, about Europe, and about eternity." Mr. Raleigh is especially good on the subject of the Middle West opposed to the East, one of the principal points of The Great Gatsby. When we have read this valuable essay we see the book as we have never quite seen it before.

And this is true of the various other novels Mr. Raleigh investigates. He makes a particularly compelling examination of The Damnation of Theron Ware, by Harold

Frederic, a novel which deserves to be better known; those who have not read it will certainly be impelled to do so after going through Mr. Raleigh's essay on it.

In the case of Thomas Mann, Mr. Raleigh usefully explicates two of that author's novels which might at first sight seem to be in most ways different: Doctor Faustus and The Holy Sinner. They are in many respects opposites, as Mr. Raleigh demonstrates, but they also have a relationship which he carefully develops.

Mr. Raleigh's range is great: he can speak with authority about both Henry James and Charles Dickens, making equally revealing comments about each. Using his historical sense, he also writes a highly entertaining, expertly documented account of the effect of Sir Walter Scott on the Victorians.

Although written at different times, these essays belong together; they comprise an important reading experience. Their author is Professor of English at the University of California, Berkeley. He has written another book for the Crosscurrents / Modern Critiques series, The Plays of Eugene O'Neill, and is also the author of Matthew Arnold and American Culture. His anthology, History and the Individual, exemplifies the working of his historical sense, so evident in the present volume and so well matched by his critical ability.

HARRY T. MOORE

Southern Illinois University
November 11, 1967

CONTENTS

INTRODUCTION

THE FOLLOWING ESSAYS were published over a period, roughly, of a decade, from the early 1950's to the early 1960's. There are statements in them to which I would perhaps no longer subscribe, or that today I would qualify, but I have left everything to stand as it was originally written. The significance of the title, "Time, Place, and Idea," to certain of the individual essays should be obvious, but there are in the book as a whole, I find retrospectively, other basic preoccupations and ideas, the most important of which have been unconscious or barely conscious. The first of these seems to be the concept of polarity, with the correlated distrust of Absolutes, in D. H. Lawrence's sense.

So, the polarity of the dynamic consciousness, from the very start of Life! Direct flowing and flashing of two consciousness streams, active in the bringing forth of an individual being. The sweet commingling, the sharp clash of opposition. And no possibility of creative development without this polarity, this dual circuit of direct, spontaneous, interchange. No hope of life apart from this. The primal unconscious pulsing in its circuits between two beings: love and wrath, cleaving and repulsion, inglutination and excrementation. What is the good of inventing "ideal" behavior?—["The Birth of Consciousness" in *Psychoanalysis and the Unconscious*, New York, 1960, p. 24]

And in some sense the novel is the prime literary instrument for expressing this sense. Thus Lawrence once more:

> The novel is a great discovery: far greater than Galileo's telescope or somebody else's wireless. The novel is the highest form of human expression so far attained. Why? Because it's incapable of the absolute.
>
> In a novel, everything is relative to everything else, if that novel is art at all.— [*The Later D. H. Lawrence*, ed. William York Tindall (New York, 1952), p. 189.]

Other great novelists have felt the same way. Thus Dostoevsky (in a letter to his brother):

> Why do you wonder about our duality. It is the commonest of human traits: my duality was throughout my life my great torment and my great delight.

Morris Cohen has said that the "Principle of Polarity" is the cutting edge of philosophical investigation, and the same is true, from my point of view, of literary investigation. Literature itself insensibly demonstrates this inherent duality. Thus the great period of the English novel, from the eighteenth to the early twentieth century, begins (Richardson and Fielding) and ends (Lawrence-Joyce) in exemplary dichotomies (the Lawrence-Joyce antithesis is discussed in chapter 8). And in the middle of these two centuries are Scott and Austen, the big "bow-wow" and the ivory carving. Or to take a single instance, the quintessential meaning of *The Damnation of Theron Ware* is expressible in an antithesis (see chapter 5). Or two novels by one writer, as with *Dr. Faustus* and *The Holy Sinner*, can have a dialectical relationship (chapter 2).

The other persistent assumption of these essays seems to be that literature and history are complementary and reflexive. Thus it is equally fruitful, in the understanding of either, to work from history to literature, as in "Victorian Morals and the Modern Novel," or to take a single instance of literature, as in the essays on *The Great Gatsby* or *The Damnation of Theron Ware*, and work outward from it into fairly large stretches of history. The relationship between history and literature is analogous to the enigmatic connection between form and content in literature itself: the two are inextricable, and the one is unthinkable without the other. If, on the one hand, no work of literature is completely comprehensible (by which I mean both the form and the content) without its historical context, on the other hand, the internal history of man is written, often in advance, as Freud among others recognized, by the great imaginative writers. Thus when the inevitable Russian Revolution finally erupted in its final form in 1917, the intelligentsia said: "It happened according to Dostoevsky." Ezra Pound has said that writers are the antennae of the race, and I believe history bears him out.

But literature has much to do with life, that is, ordinary experience, or, to put it another way, it helps in that never-ending, never fully-realizable, process of finding out what we are, and, to a certain extent, what we must do. Not that literature is "moral" in any direct or simple fashion. I, at least, have never met any saintly types—and there are some—who got that way from reading books, nor has anyone ever been struck by the overwhelming incidence of magnanimity, liberality, largeness of vision, humaneness, generosity and simple Christian charity displayed by literary or humanistic people, who seem to bear in their breasts as much malice as the rest of the human race. Further, solitary studies, which is what humanistic studies are, with their concomitant burden of introspection, do not lead one to take a charitable view of oneself, much less the rest of the human race. Nor does serious literature itself either demonstrate or certify the "morality" of mankind.

What literature does, first, is to disclose the possibilities of human life, as no other medium does, and therefore it can widen, and deepen, human consciousness. It is "vicarious" (in the nonpejorative sense) experience of a high and subtle order. It does not please by "instruction" but by "complication." Furthermore, it has a dialectical relationship to the human psyche in that, as Edmund Wilson says, one never reads the same book twice, for each time through, or around, a reverberating book, one's own self has changed; so that the preceding reading is a memory, like other memories, and the present experience is "fresh," sometimes in quite surprising ways. Finally, if man has some kind of nature, which has never been proven or demonstrated, and human experience has some kind of meaning, a moot point once more, literature, while "proving" nothing in itself, is extremely potent evidence in any serious investigation of these two propositions. It should be among the first of the relevant human agencies or institutions called in to testify (and of course it would be found to be on both sides of both arguments).

So, at the last, one never gets to the bottom of the province of literature, especially as it ramifies out into philosophy, psychology, the fine arts, sociology, history, even the natural sciences. The simple physical, or physiological, task alone of reading, in a single life-time, all one should read is insuperable. As for the meaning of it all, *that* stretches out into infinity. We are all humble workers in the vineyard, but the vineyard is real and the work, however small in the large perspective, is worth the while.

For permission to use articles, the author and publisher are grateful to the Modern Language Association of America for "Henry James: The Poetics of Empiricism," *The Sewanee Review* for "The English Novel and the Three Kinds of Time," Duke University Press (*American Literature*) for "*The Damnation of Theron Ware*," *Victorian Studies* for "What Scott Meant to the Victorians," *Nineteenth-Century Fiction* for "Dickens and the Sense of Time," *The Pacific Spectator* for "Mann's Double Vision: *Doctor Faustus* and The Holy Sinner," *University Review* for "Fitzgerald's *The Great Gatsby*: Legendary Bases and Allegorical Significances," and *Partisan Review* for "Victorian Morals and the Modern Novel."

JOHN HENRY RALEIGH

Berkeley, California
December 22, 1966

Time, Place, and Idea

1   HENRY JAMES
THE POETICS OF EMPIRICISM

CRITICISM OF HENRY JAMES in our time is verging into metaphysics. The late works have recently been analyzed in terms of "dialectic" and "myth," [1] as products of Swedenborgianism,[2] and as an artistic objectification of William James's philosophical pragmatism.[3] Despite great individual differences these three approaches hold in common the basic assumption that James's inner and final meaning has not yet been ascertained and the corollary assumption that this final meaning is perhaps expressed symbolically, by technique, rather than overtly by subject matter.[4] In this climate of opinion James is conceived of as a kind of nineteenth-century Dante, the architect of a secular *Divine Comedy* for some later-day equivalent of scholasticism, and the legendary "late manner," once considered merely idiosyncratic, is thought to be an elaborate structure which metaphorically expresses a coherent system of values. The critical problems are, first, to find James's Aquinas, or the rationale for the body of ideas on which the late works constitute a metaphor, and, second, to define the relationship between this logical statement and James's symbolic one.

The following essay will proceed along these lines. Although I have no St. Thomas to offer, I should like to point out some broad but unmistakable analogies between the basic characteristics of James's work as a whole and a certain body of ideas, whose ultimate source will be briefly sketched, and to suggest, further, that the late technique is an esthetic embodiment of these ideas. In terms of the evolution of James's art, with which this essay will also be concerned, my thesis is that the mature technique simply makes explicit certain distinctive qualities which are implicit in all the novels, early and late.

James, of all novelists, must be approached obliquely, and his "distinctive qualities" are best defined in a formal rather than in a subjective manner. As generations of irritated readers attest, James's novels are not case histories of human beings whom one can talk about as of one's friends; but, at the same time, these novels constitute, collectively, a perfectly valid interpretation of and a remarkable metaphor on human experience in general. With James, as indeed with any other novelist, there can be no simple equation of art to life, for characters in a novel are not human and there is no *necessary* direct connection between them and us. A connection may exist but it is fortuitous rather than logical since they are motivated not by our own sometimes unique drives or peculiar experiences but by certain assumptions that the author holds, consciously or unconsciously, as to what constitutes personality, experience, and their interaction. Thus, like a philosopher he is trying with aid of certain theoretical assumptions to impose form and meaning on the chaos of life; and his characters are not human beings but meaning-functions within this system. It is from their consonance with the system and not ourselves that they derive their validity. In James's novels, his most memorable or remarkable characters, like Isabel Archer or Strether, are those who most perfectly body forth his basic assumptions as to the nature of personality and experience.

All this is obvious and, perhaps, presents no great problem in the earlier nineteenth-century novel where the depiction is all done by an omniscient author, who tells you what to think, and where the action is liable to be external rather than internal, making it necessary for the reader himself to supply much of the motivation. But when the author moves out of the way, and the novel itself becomes introspective, as with James, then the subject matter becomes that most inexplicable of all subjects, human consciousness, and necessarily the author must have fairly definite ideas as to its nature and function or he could bring no order at all to his art.

Using the word "idea" in connection with James is perhaps misleading. Strictly speaking he had none, or at least he professed to have none. His father's philosophy, in fact any abstract system, possibly excepting his brother William's, left him cold. T. S. Eliot in one of his famous pronouncements has said that James's mind was too fine ever to be violated by an abstraction; and, in a sense, Eliot is right. James did entertain ideas, but they only filtered in obliquely through the maze of personal relationships and feeling-values which for him constituted the basic ingredient of life itself and the subject-matter of his novels. But he did have an abiding conviction, which was that human consciousness was beatitude, the only real value in a complex, almost indecipherable universe, and the sole argument for immortality. This was his real subject matter, and the late works, in effect, comprise a religion of consciousness. Page after page is given to its exploration; characters are ranked according to how high or how low, in perceptiveness and subtlety, are their conscious minds; and the movement of the story progresses as various bundles of consciousness impinge upon one another, attracted or repulsed or drifting. Thus James's system, since I have now made him a metaphysician, has at its heart a certain attitude toward, and hence certain assumptions about, consciousness. These assumptions determine the generic qualities of life-experience in James's novels. The critical problem then is to comprehend and define as closely as possible the nature of this "consciousness" which gives meaning to the works.

There are certain fundamental traits in all the Jamesian characters and the life they lead that have been noted by many critics: their passivity, their sensitivity, their acquisitiveness, their individualism, the ambiguous quality of their motivations which are always concerned with ethical choice but never have reference to an explicit moral code, their supreme esthetic sense which seems to encompass all aspects of their personality, their subtle, complex, but constantly shifting interdependence, one with another, and, finally, the tenuous nature of everything, where hardly any problem is completely clear-cut, no relationship ever certain or immutable, no issue ever precisely decided.

Many of these characteristics can be and have been accounted for by critics in sociological terms. For example, individualism and acquisitiveness are pre-eminently American traits and to point this out is to say that the novels of James reflect the culture into which he was born. But the passivity and the tenuous and ambiguous quality of experience are hardly accounted for by a comparison with nineteenth-century American society, and it is these two traits which so distinguish James's vision of life. Very often they are explained away in Freudian terms and are taken to be an unconscious expression of James's own sexual aberration, whatever it was. But the reduction of the novels to an end-product of this condition is as fallacious as the view that holds Dostoevsky's works to be solely the eruptions of an epileptic. Both of these great and distinctive novelists wrote as they did because they were so deeply expressive of their respective cultures. By the time of his death Dostoevsky was rightly regarded as one of the national prophets. Posthumously, James is beginning to be accorded the same rank, and with some justice, for the distinctive characteristics of human experience in James's novels, passivity and ambiguity, have their root and source in a group of ideas profoundly fundamental to American culture.

As every textbook says, the ideas of British empiricism are basic to most American institutions and to the American life-attitude in its theory if not always in its practice. The dismissal of absolutes, the political democracy, the social equality, the religious tolerance, the moral relativity, the personal individualism, the respect for property, all these fundamental traits and many more have been shown to be implicit in the thinking of Locke and his successors. It is a gross oversimplification, of course, to say that there is a straight line between Locke's ideas and American culture. Many factors, including the whole history and heritage of Western civilization, the geography of the American continent, the personal motives of the men who founded its institutions, enter in, but it is reasonable to assume that the doctrines of Locke were primary here and found congenial surroundings. And, in spite of Transcendentalism and the other great forces abroad in nineteenth-century America, a substratum of Lockeanism persisted, as Merle Curti [5] has effectively demonstrated. Constantly, in sermons, in Fourth of July orations, and in other public speeches Locke or his doctrines were referred to or quoted. If anything, the extreme individualism of British empiricism, enshrined originally in the Constitution and in various social institutions, became more radical in its American setting. In a Fourth of July oration, delivered at Newport in 1861, Henry James Sr. gave voice to the common feeling that in the United States the twin bases of individualism, Protestantism and constitutional liberty, which had been inherited from England and for which Locke was prime philosophical spokesman, would finally reach full fruition in his own native land: "We inherit Protestantism and constitutional liberty; but there is a vast difference between us and them, *we begin where they leave off* . . . they affirm the inalienable sanctity and freedom of the nation as against other nations; we, the inalienable sanctity and freedom of the subject as against the nation." [6]

Now behind these familiar democratic sentiments lay certain assumptions about the nature of man, and, as Henry James Sr. was a vigorous expositor of these assumptions in political and social terms, so Henry Jr., perhaps quite unwittingly, constructed his novels on their psychological premises. This relationship will perhaps be more clear if I set forth very briefly Locke's fundamental assumptions concerning personality and experience, well-known in a general sense but not, so far as I know, in this particular context.

In Locke's philosophy [7] the basic entity of man was a

mental substance, which was at once different in kind from all material substances, such as the body and the physical universe, and, at the same time, independent of and separate from all other mental substances. On a material level, this mental substance, using an aggregate of material substances, such as the body and tools, acquired other material substances, or property, which then assumed a status coequal to that of the body itself. On the conscious level, the mental substance was a blank consciousness, the tabula rasa, which received impressions from and thus perceived qualities in material objects. These qualities were either primary, inherent in the object; secondary, inherent in the perceptor; or tertiary, inherent in neither. Most of the impressions were secondary or sensory. The blank was nothing in itself but did have the power of reflection which enabled it to develop epistemologically by the process of abstraction, turning particular impressions into general ideas.

Practically every character trait and every interrelationship in the James novels can be accounted for as the logical outcome of these ideas. For example, if the basic element of man, the mental substance, is different from and independent of all material substances, including its own body, then it follows that here alone a knowable reality exists; hence James's exclusive concern with his characters' consciousness, to the exclusion of anything materially concrete about them, including their own physical passions. Again if all these mental substances are independent of one another and possess no innate ideas in common, then there is no specified or specifiable relationship between them, and their moral relationships become a highly individualistic affair. Each person is his own arbiter and must arrive at moral decisions by an appeal to his own experience, which, in this case, usually means sense impressions, and, finally, morality becomes purely esthetic. The consciousness most sensitive to impressions is liable to be the most moral. So in James there is an equation between the esthetic and the moral sense, and the individual who most appreciates the beauty of a Renaissance painting is also the most moral. Or to consider the attitude toward material things. If material substances, or property, assume a status equal to that of the body, they are then an extension of that body, and ownership becomes sacrosanct. So the Ververs of *The Golden Bowl,* inordinately acquisitive in any literal sense, are presented in the Jamesian context as admirably disinterested people, and, generally, in the world of James no opprobrium attaches to what might be regarded as the most blatant materialism. Very often those that have the most, Newman, Isabel Archer, Milly Theale, the Ververs, are also the most admirable since they are expressing themselves most fully. The characters of *The Spoils of Poynton* are ranked according to how finely they appreciate the "spoils." Conversely, evil and corruption usually set in when the dispossessed, like Gilbert Osmond or Kate Croy, reach out for their share. But the corruption is in them, in their lack of perception, not in the fact of materialism itself. There are many other analogies that could be drawn between the assumptions of empirical philosophy and the works of James, and most of them would probably be true of many other English and American novelists as well. But there are two implications of Lockeanism which seem to have been most vividly realized in James's works and which, in turn, give the works their uniqueness, for, without Freudianizing James, one can show that both the passivity of his characters and the ambiguity of their relationships are the logical outcome of the empirical assumptions on consciousness, personality, and experience.

This perhaps sounds too simple to be true but James's beloved consciousness, the chief subject matter of his works, was nothing more than an artistic presentation of the idea of the tabula rasa being written upon by experience, or sense impressions. If the mind is a blank upon which experience writes, then it follows that personality itself is passive rather than active and that a person is more of an observer than anything else; consequently there is that thin red line of sad young men in the James novels who rise to life's battle only to renounce, and the archetypal figure, Isabel Archer or Strether, is the perfect observer upon whom nothing is lost. Not all the Jamesian characters are atrophied by their passivity; a character such as Newman, who, in Locke's words, has "mixed his labor with" the wilderness, has a powerful will and a capacity for action, but everybody's inner life, which is the subject matter of most of the late works, is invariably presented as passive rather than active, as compared, for instance, to the inner life of a Stephen Dedalus or a Raskolnikov. Very often this passivity is liable to encompass the outer life as well.

Ambiguity in human relationships is likewise a logical implication of empirical psychology. If each mental substance is absolutely independent of every other mental substance and they are all equal, they can be organized in no objective fashion, such as hierarchically, and there can be no specified relationship between them. Their relationships then must necessarily be ambiguous: so in James there are the frankly ambiguous conclusions to *The Portrait of a Lady* and *The Wings of the Dove*; a margin of obscurity in most of the relationships of the later works, as, for instance, in *The Spoils of Poynton* where only omniscience itself could ever satisfactorily figure out what happened and why; and, finally, an essential isolation of all characters illustrated thematically by the betrayal motif that runs through all the novels and exemplified constantly by the conscious processes of the characters, most of whom are eternally engaged in the ever-changing, never-ending task of trying to figure out their inexplicable fellow characters.

These general characteristics, passivity of the individual mind and ambiguity in human relations, are evident in both the early and late works of James, but they are much more marked in the late. This was not brought about by perversity on James's part, as has often been charged, but by the fact that his technique had become completely functional and spoke these basic characteristics in style and structure as well as in theme and action. One hesitates to add anything to the literature about that monumental phenomenon, the late style. Many explanations have been given, each having a claim to validity. It is said that the habit of dictation, the theatrical experiences, various literary influences, such as Conrad, Maeterlinck, and Ibsen, all contributed to the increasing elaboration of the late works. But it is also assumed that James had somehow arrived at a "deeper psychology" and that the late characters are more profoundly conceived or more profoundly probed than the earlier ones. To the contrary, there is an almost unholy consistency in the general traits of the Jamesian characters as a whole, from early period to later. Newman of *The American,* early, and Adam Verver of *The Golden Bowl,* late, are fundamentally similar in basic make-up. Both are misrepresentations of the self-made American millionaire of the nineteenth century, a familiar figure in all of James's novels—morally superior, extremely sensitive, inordinately curious, a supreme gatherer of impressions, in short, a superior tabula rasa linked to an American will and capacity for practical action. Minus the capacity for practical action and hence the wealth, Strether of *The Ambassadors* is essentially the same type. This broad equation of Newman to Verver to Strether is not meant to imply that James did not vary his types; rather it suggests that the infinite variations were played, as they always are, on certain great and basic themes, here the fundamental assumptions of empiricism concerning personality, experience, and the conscious life.

Yet there is an enormous difference between Newman and Verver in their respective contexts, and the difference is, once more, the difference of technique. If there is a change in psychological portrayal, it is one of extension rather than depth; that is, the characters and their reactions to situations are the same but James has deepened and enriched their *effect* on the reader by all the resources of the late style, and the greater part of the power of the late style results from the fact that the concepts of consciousness which in the early novels were only vaguely implicit in the characters and their situations have now become explicit in the style. This increased immediacy of effect in the late style has been partly accounted for by what is called the method of "dramatization." In the mature period, James, instead of analytically describing his characters, presented directly the workings of their minds. This presentation was always carefully controlled and ordered, as he wished to avoid the uncontrolled flux of real experience, but it accomplished the aim of presenting a version of experience directly to the reader. Nevertheless, even admitting the gains in immediacy assured by this device, one may still be baffled by the peculiar splendor of the conscious lives and by the subtly shifting relationships of the characters in *The Wings of the Dove* and *The Golden Bowl.*

The point I am trying to make can best be illustrated by a comparison of James's handling of the same psychological process, the conscious mental substance being acted upon, at three different stages of his career, early, middle, and late. Newman of *The American,* Hyacinth Robinson of *The Princess Casamassima,* and Maggie Verver of *The Golden Bowl* are all typical in that they operate, psychologically, in the same fashion, and, by a comparison of each in the process of being conscious, the functional nature of the late technique is underlined. *The American* was written early, in a straightforward fashion and a simple style. We are told, directly and initially, of the receptivity of Newman: "It [Newman's face] had that paucity of detail, which is not yet emptiness, that blankness which is not simplicity, that look of being committed to nothing in particular, of standing in a posture of general hospitality to the chances of life, of being very much at one's own disposal, characteristic of American faces of the clear strain." [8] Now Newman in a moment of crisis when his intended bride, Madame de Cintré, has told him that she is to become a Carmelite nun: "The image rose there, at her words, too dark and horrible for belief, and affected him as if she had told him she was going to mutilate her beautiful face or drink some potion that would make her mad" (II, 418). There is nothing particularly distinctive about this, and the image comes in on the receptor in conventional terms of horror.

With Hyacinth Robinson of *The Princess Casamassima* the psychological process, while basically the same, is beginning to acquire power and depth. James had not yet arrived at the fullfledged dramatic method; so much about Hyacinth is described rather than presented, but the description is becoming fuller, more elaborate, and more concrete. The comparison between Newman and Robinson is, perhaps, not apt, since they are radically different social types. Newman is an American millionaire and Robinson an impoverished English bookbinder, but Hyacinth demonstrates the general direction in which James was traveling in describing the mind being operated upon. This is Hyacinth's consciousness after he has begun his apprenticeship as a bookmaker:

> For this unfortunate but remarkably-organized youth every displeasure or gratification of the visual sense coloured his whole mind, and though he lived in Pentonville and worked in Soho, though he was poor and obscure and cramped and full of unattainable desires, nothing in life had such an interest or such a price for him as his impressions and reflexions. They came from everything he touched, they made him vibrate, kept him thrilled and throbbing, for most of his waking consciousness, and they constituted as yet the principal events and stages of his career [v, 159].

As the book goes on, Hyacinth's mind begins to get dramatized, in the late manner, and the metaphors of this dramatization begin to dazzle in the late manner. When he returns, dubiously, to his work, after a sojourn on the continent, "He gave a little private groan of relief when he discovered that he still liked his work and that the thriving swarm of his ideas in the matters of order and books returned to him. They came in still brighter, more suggestive form, and he had the satisfaction of feeling that his taste had improved" (vi, 155). Still later the process begins to sound the organ-note:

> The influence of his permeating London had closed over him again; Paris and Milan and Venice had shimmered away into reminiscence and picture; and as the great city which was most his lay around him under her pall like an

immeasurable breathing monster he felt with vague excitement, as he had felt before, only now with more knowledge, that it was the richest expression of the life of man. His horizon had been immensely widened, but it was filled again by the expanse that sent dim night-gleams and strange, blurred reflexions and emanations into a sky without stars. He suspended, so to say, his small sensibility in the midst of it, to quiver there with joy and hope and ambition as well as with the effort of renunciation [vi, 266].

To move now to *The Golden Bowl* and Maggie Verver *not* having an experience, in a famous metaphor (she is speculating upon her problem, an unfaithful husband and a faithless friend):

She might fairly, as she watched them, have missed it as a lost thing; have yearned for it, for the straight vindictive view, the rights of resentment, the rages of jealousy, the protests of passion, as for something she had been cheated of not least: a range of feelings which for many women would have meant so much, but which for *her* husband's wife, for her father's daughter, figured nothing nearer to experience than a wild eastern caravan, looming into view with crude colours in the sun, fierce pipes in the air, high spears against the sky, all a thrill, a natural joy to mingle with, but turning off short before it reached her and plunging into other defiles (xxiv, 236–37).

And, as *The Golden Bowl* progresses towards its climax, the images become successively more savage; thus before one of the great showdowns with her husband's mistress Maggie is shown walking on the terrace: "The hour was moonless and starless and the air heavy and still—which was why, in her evening dress, she need feel no chill and could get away, in the outer darkness, from that provocation of opportunity which had assaulted her, within, on her sofa, as a beast might have leaped at her throat" (xxiv, 235). Or she compares herself to "the night-watcher in a beast-haunted land who has no more means for fire" (xxiv, 299–300).

These three illustrations, chosen, naturally, to prove my

point, but not misrepresentative of the general development of James's style, point up the difference between
incoming impressions in the early and late novels: formerly they are conventionally imaged; latterly they actually assault, and thus give the effect to the reader of
"depth." The purest expression of all this is probably in
The Beast in the Jungle, a late nouvelle, in which experience is pictured as a crouching beast ready to spring.
Ironically enough, the beast never springs, until it is too
late, on the protagonist, John Marcher, who was "the man
of his time, *the* man, to whom nothing on earth was to
have happened" (XVII, 125). Marcher's personal tragedy is
that he does not take the love offered to him by a woman
whom, he realizes too late, he loved. His metaphysical
tragedy, in the context of the idea of the tabula rasa, is
that since nothing has ever happened to him the blank
remains a blank and thus has no meaning; so Marcher, in
a sense, does not even exist as a personality, and his
impression on the reader suggests precisely that. Of course
not all impressions in the late novels leap like beasts at
their receptor. Sometimes they caress, as in the great water
metaphors when, in stasis, characters sink into a massive
sea. The important thing to remember is that they are
invariably physically imaged; and thus practically all feelings, love, or hate, or fear, are pictured as a series of sense
impressions coming in upon the consciousness.

The idea that the mind is a blank upon which experience writes is certainly not peculiar to British empiricism—it can be found in Aristotle—nor is James the only
novelist ever to conceive of experience in these terms. But
the stress which empirical philosophy puts on sense
impressions, pure and simple, and on the initial blankness
and passivity of the mind is unique, and James also is
unique in carrying this idea to its logical extreme and
poeticizing it in such terms of splendor. As might be
expected, James had the defects of his virtues. Gide,
among many, has pointed out that the James characters
have no subconscious and "seem never to exist except in
the functioning of their intellects." [9] Thus a Strether com-

pared to a Raskolnikov or a Dedalus may seem thin, and of course he is, the difference between James and such novelists as Dostoevsky and Joyce being the distance between the tabula rasa and Freud's subconscious. Against the "swarm of ideas" that "return" to Hyacinth Robinson, one might juxtapose the following quotation from Dostoevsky's *The Possessed*: it is Lyamshin cogitating: "A swarm of ideas flared up in Lyamshin's crafty mind like a shower of fireworks." [10]

But it is significant that James was reaching out, near the end of his career, to a more complex view of personality. In *The Jolly Corner* the protagonist develops an alter ego and in *The Sense of the Past* he exchanges personalities with a dead ancestor. Edmund Wilson has pointed out that Dickens was working toward the same thing late in his career, especially in the unfinished *The Mystery of Edwin Drood*.[11] Wilson concluded that social pressures prevented Dickens from ever exploring personality in the uncompromising terms of Dostoevsky. In James's case, I should say that he would have been prevented the ultimate realization of a depth psychology by his own assumptions about consciousness. So in *The Jolly Corner* and in *The Sense of the Past* the alter egos have to be actually objectified and placed in other bodies, rather than erupting from within the protagonist himself, as in Freudian psychology. James, like all major artists, carried his medium as far as it would go, and, in the final climacteric, was stretching it to express the inexpressible. It was as if James from the simple beginnings of conventional narrative in the early works had gradually sunk deeper and deeper into the personality, empirically conceived. In full maturity he was able to invest this concept with great splendor as for example in the description of the mind of Frank Saltram in *The Coxon Fund*: "The sight of a great, suspended, swinging crystal,—huge, lucid, lustrous, a block of light—flashing back every impression of life and every possibility of thought" (xv, 300). But James had sounded the limits, and in his late career he seemed to be trying to go beyond. And for the reader there is often in the very late novels, as in *The Sense of the Past,* a sense of strain, as if the medium were being stretched to the point of cracking and were constantly threatening to double back and parody itself. But despite these attempts the consciousness of the characters and their reaction to experience remained the tabula rasa being bombarded by sense impressions and passively reworking these into knowledge.

The most effective demonstration of this is contained in the nouvelle *In the Cage.* The protagonist, a telegraph-office operator, works, literally, in a cage. She is from the lower classes, but James is careful to endow her with a sensibility superior to her kind, and she is another perfect observer and a superior recording apparatus. Infernally sensitive and infernally acute, she lives a vicarious existence, sitting passively in her cage, in the lives of telegram-senders, most of whom are from the upper classes and are carrying on adulterous intrigues. Outside the cage she has a life of her own, a family and a fiancé, but James makes it clear that her real life goes on in the cage: "She had surrendered herself moreover of late to a certain expansion of her consciousness; something that seemed perhaps vulgarly accounted for by the fact that, as the blast of the season roared louder and the waves of fashion passed their spray further over the counter, there were more impressions to be gathered and really—for it came to that—more *life to be led* [italics mine]" (xi, 373–74). Later on James describes how these impressions are transmuted into knowledge. The girl is visiting a sea resort with her fiancé, a superior grocer; they go to hear a band concert and the forthright grocer, Mr. Mudge, wishes to mingle with the crowd and approach the band-stand, but she, and this is significant, prefers the periphery, "the far end, away from the band and the crowd; as to which she had frequent differences with her friend, who reminded her often that they could have only in the thick of it the sense of the money they were getting back. That had little effect on her, for she got back her money by seeing many things, the things of the past year, fall together and connect themselves, undergo the happy relegation that transforms melancholy and misery, passion and effort, into experience and knowledge" (XI, 452).

Turning from the treatment of individual minds and the question of style to the treatment of individual relationships and the question of structure, one finds, again, that the technique of the late works is an attempt to dramatize most effectively the essential ambiguity of these relationships within which the various characters are, paradoxically, both intimately intertwined and utterly isolated, and where each individual can know another only from moment to moment and then never completely.

This tenuous quality of character relationships is most obviously illustrated by James's practice of sometimes leaving his story hanging in air, with no absolute conclusion. At the end of *The Portrait of a Lady* we know that Isabel is to return to her villainous husband, but at the same time Henrietta Stackpole tells Caspar Goodwood that his cause is not wholly lost. This, however, is of small comfort to Goodwood. The reader does not know for sure whether Henrietta is right or wrong, or whether Caspar will resign or continue his pursuit. Conscious of his own assumptions here, James wrote, in the preface to *Roderick Hudson*: "Really, universally, relations stop nowhere, and the exquisite problem of the artist is eternally but to draw, by a geometry of his own, the circle within which they shall happily *appear* to do so" (I, vii). But even the geometry of the artist is not capable of always drawing a closed circle, as the ambiguous conclusion of *The Wings of the Dove* attests. The ambiguity, to be sure, is not total. When Kate Croy says to Merton Densher in the last sentence of the book: "We shall never be again as we were!" the reader realizes that their relationship has been altered by the tragic death of Milly Theale, whom they had both betrayed, and that, in some way, her superior morality has mitigated their own amorality. But the exact nature of the change is never described, nor is their future relationship specified. The circle, in other words, is left open. Theoretically, as James himself realized when he used the word "universal" in connection with human relations, his novels should not have been finite, for relationships always change and never end, barring death, and thus never reach a definite and immutable "rapport." Joyce said that, ideally, he should have liked to compress everything he had to say into one word which would then be his total work; working in just the opposite direction, toward infinite linguistic expansion, James, in an ideal situation, should have taken a single set of relationships and have gone on writing about them eternally. In the late novels, according to many readers, he almost achieves this end.

Even when the circle is closed, as it often is, there is generally a margin of obscurity in character motivation in the story itself. One could easily go insane trying to ascertain what has happened in *The Sacred Fount*. To a lesser degree the same is true of most of the later works, where the characters are, in the last analysis, fundamentally isolated from and ignorant of one another. The isolation is symbolized most tragically by the betrayal theme, the "Judas complex," that runs through all the works, early and late, but which is usually presented most starkly in the late period. Thus Milly Theale, dying, betrayed and alone in a Venetian palace, turns her face to the wall and dies, and Maggie Verver, utterly isolated because of her ignorance of life and of the real nature of the people around her, faces for the first time the fact of evil in human relationships.

Nor is it merely coincidental that so many characters in James's novels are solitaries with only the vaguest of antecedents. Even the forthright Newman is given a past of hints and shades, and he, evidently, has no ties or connections. In what I regard as James's masterpiece, *The Wings of the Dove*, each of the principals is carefully introduced as an isolated figure. Kate Croy, to be sure, has friends and family, but on none can she rely. Living in her aunt's house, she is described, in battle terms, as one besieged by her "lioness" aunt (xix, 29–30). Densher, her lover-to-be, appears upon the scene, a man of rootless bringing-up, vaguely continental. He is a bachelor, having neither family nor friends. Milly Theale is presented as being the very last of a once great family, and she, like Densher, is utterly alone. Her companion and confidante, Susan Stringer, is a widow and a solitary. A sense of fluidity and isolation pervades the whole book. Kate and Merton in conversation are described as occupying a "small floating island" (XIX, 66). Milly is a great steamer drawing the little boat of Susan Stringer in her wake (XIX, 113). In essence, the novel is set in motion as these more or less isolated mental substances come together to become interlaced about their moral problem.

Emphasizing the isolation of the Jamesian characters is their essential ignorance of one another. This is conveyed structurally by the device of the point of view, whereby, even if the point of view shifts from one person to another, no one person is ever in complete possession of all the facts. The reader may perhaps be able to add everything up but not necessarily so, as the conclusion to *The Wings of the Dove* attests. Very often the late works tend to become, structurally speaking, essays on the frailty of human intercourse. The movement of *The Golden Bowl* progresses as various characters make sallies into the vast unknown which is themselves and their mutual situation. It takes a whole book for Maggie to realize that her husband and her father's wife are lovers, another book for her to convey her knowledge of this to all the principals and bring on the dénouement. Within this dimly-lit circle, there are various greater or lesser degrees of ignorance. Mrs. Assingham, the observer, knows more than Maggie at first but does not know that Maggie will ultimately rise to the problem and settle it. Charlotte, the friend, finally realizes that Maggie knows of the situation but underestimates her intelligence and assumes that Maggie can do nothing. Maggie thinks that her father does not know, but he does and, in turn, thinks she does not. This stops all real communication between them, as they protect one another's supposed ignorance. Finally, at the end, by an esoteric sign—nothing is ever explicitly said—they convey their mutual knowledge to one another, as the novel ends.

Yet, despite their isolation and their ignorance of one another, the characters of these novels are subtly and intimately interconnected in an eternally fluid relationship, coming together to shoot impressions at one another, drifting apart to rework the impressions into knowledge and coming together again in a different relationship. This sense of fluidity is often carried over into the physical action itself, and characters are fluidly attracted and repelled. In *The Golden Bowl* Charlotte is seen by Maggie as a free-ranging and feline animal: "The splendid shining supple creature was out of the cage, was at large; and the question now almost grotesquely rose of whether she mightn't by some art, just where she was and before she could go further, be hemmed in and secured" (xxiv, 239). Later the pair slowly drift together:

> Charlotte, extending her search, appeared now to define herself vaguely in the distance; of this after an instant the Princess was sure, though the darkness was thick, for the projected clearness of the smoking-room windows had presently contributed its help. Her friend came slowly into that circle having also, for herself, by this time, not indistinguishably discovered that Maggie was on the terrace. Maggie, from the end, saw her stop before one of the windows to look at the group within, and then saw her come nearer and pause again, still with a considerable length of the place between them [xxiv, 241].

Needless to say, several pages pass before the slow envelopment is completed and the two confront one another.

The fluid nature of the action, combined with the passivity of the characters, almost gives one the feeling that the only objective and solid entity is the problem itself, whatever it may be, and that it, in a sense, dominates the action. Stransom of *The Altar of the Dead* is described as moving "round and round" a problem "in widening circles" (xvii, 44) and in all the late works, the characters continually circle situations which assail them with impressions. The situation or the problem is always themselves and the complex of their relations, but it invariably seems to take on a life of its own. In *The Golden Bowl* the situation is actually symbolized by the bowl with the concealed flaw. So too, in most of the late works, one has the feeling that in the center of the room, dominating all, as it shoots its impressions out to the various mental substances who drift around it, repulsed or attracted, is the sole objective entity, the problem itself. It is somewhat like Locke's primary quality, whose nature the observer arrives at by a succession of sense impressions or secondary qualities.

In short, the action in a late James novel is inherently anarchic, for isolation of the individual and ambiguity in human relationships are but the logical and final outcome of James's fundamental psychological premise, Locke's free-wheeling mental substance. Significantly, although perhaps quite coincidentally, James chose the anarchist movement to portray in his political novel *The Princess Casamassima*, and in his personal life, as his secretary Theodora Bosanquet tells us, he became, in the late years, more and more of an absolute individualist: "His Utopia was an anarchy where nobody would be responsible for any human being but only for his own civilized character." [12] Correspondingly, in the mature technique, personal relationships became more fluid and ambiguous, understanding of one character by another more difficult and problematical, and the conscious mental process of each individual, now thrown back completely on himself or herself, more spectacular and vivid. The "late manner" seems to have been an elaborate subterfuge, sometimes conceived with mathematical precision, as in *The Golden Bowl*, to impose order on this human situation which was continually threatening to dissolve into atomism.

Taken in this sense James's novels are prophetic, an esthetic counterpart to so many American political and social institutions. To state it negatively, the anarchic individualism, the lack of close and rich social relationships, the absence of great depth in the version of life portrayed by the James novels are precisely the same traits so many foreign visitors have mentioned, disparagingly, in their assessments of American culture. Indeed many of the social observations of foreign visitors, especially in the nineteenth century, might well be read as literary criticism of James. James himself, especially in the famous *Hawthorne* passage where he laments the insubstantiality of American society and, by implication, apostrophizes England, was one of the most severe critics of his native land and its atomistic culture, but, in a deeper sense than even he realized, he never left home.

These speculations on the relationship between the logical and metaphorical statement of the same complex of ideas are not meant to turn their subject into a philosopher but to demonstrate the fact that a completely functional artistic technique is, in a sense, conceptual. In James's case it is not at all extravagant to say that his true meaning *is* his technique, which has a grammar, rhetoric, and logic beyond and above the "subject matter" of his novels and stories.

A concluding reference to philosophy is pertinent. According to Susanne Langer [13] a habit of thought reveals itself not by the answers it gives but by the questions it asks. A question is merely an ambiguous proposition for which a certain number of answers, or completions, is possible, and to ask a question is to make an assumption. For example, when the pre-Socratics speculated about the nature of matter, they necessarily made the basic assumption that there was such a thing as matter. This mode of asking questions or handling problems is the basic determinant of a system of thought and is called its "technique."

Applying this line of reasoning, by analogy, to literary criticism and to the familiar problem of the relationship between form and content, one might say that James's basic habit of thought was his complex of assumptions about the nature of human consciousness, the way it operated, and the manner in which various entities of consciousness acted upon and were related to one another. In his long career James handled many themes: the struggle of the individual for self-fulfillment and moral certitude, the impact of Europe upon the visiting American, the love between men and women, the plight of the artist, and so on. But he always asked his "questions" and thus gave his "answers" in a certain manner—roughly in terms of the assumptions of empiricism concerning personality and experience and their interaction—and this was his "technique."

MANN'S DOUBLE VISION
      DOCTOR FAUSTUS
      AND *THE HOLY SINNER* [1]

> *Of a lack of naïveté I would not speak, for in the end naïveté lies at the bottom of being, all being, even the most conscious and complicated.—Serenus Zeitblom in* Doctor Faustus

SOME REVIEWS OF Mann's latest novel, *The Holy Sinner*, while paying due credit to its extravagant charm, have exhibited a tendency, overt or covert, to dismiss the book as a *jeu d'esprit*, without serious content or meaning and to be written down as a hiatus rather than a link in Mann's evolution as a writer-thinker. And in fact this reaction to *The Holy Sinner*, while in error as I hope to demonstrate, is almost inevitable, given, first, the manner of the novel's narration and, second, the nature of contemporary literary and psychological standards.

The narration itself—the novel as story, pure and simple—is so utterly captivating that there is a tendency for any reader to go no further into the meanings of the book and to be impatient or skeptical of any other reader who would. Certain passages excepted, one can almost imagine the novel on the shelf with Dickens, to be read, chapter by chapter, to the children at bedtime. The plot has everything that the childish heart could desire: pageantry, war, a siege, individual combat, long absences and final "recognitions," a seventeen years' penance on a stone, bleeding lambs appearing to Roman patricians, involvement with all levels of society, from highest to lowest, movements over large areas of Western Europe, and, finally, a magnificently happy ending—all this conjured up by a master storyteller. The plot line is veritably Dickensian—a collection of incredible events whose very monstrousness is enchanting because we always feel that they are steadily marching forward, like orderly little soldiers, to a high and happy ending.

Even the un-Dickensian double (or is it triple?) incest, as it is presented here with a singular blend of childish piety and sophisticated irony, carries with it that aura of naïve anomalousness that so characterizes the mind of the child and through the exercise of which the child will call its father the "father" of its (the child's) mother and will almost inevitably refer to the wife as the "mother" of her husband. No young child—although its elders would not view this reaction with complacency—would be seriously disturbed by the fact that Princess Sibylla is aunt-mother-wife to the nephew-son-husband of Gregory; in fact the child might well regard such economy as admirable. Furthermore, Mann plays up these anomalies by deliberately stating and restating them in as fantastic a fashion as possible. After the original incestuous act between brother and sister, Clemens, the narrator, denominates the forthcoming issue as the son of his "aunt" and "uncle." But Sieur Eisengrein, the elder statesman whom the desperate young pair call in for advice on their predicament, exclaims, upon hearing of the incestuous fruit: "Oh, dear noble children, how bad! Here you have quite actually slept with each other so that the brother's fruit waxes in the sister's little belly and you have made your blessed father on both sides a father-in-law as well as a grandfather, all in a very irregular way." Still later, after Gregory has grown and compounded the incest by marrying his mother and having children with her, the narrator exclaims, "child of shame, his mother's spouse, his grandfather's son-in-law, his father's brother-in-law, monstrous brother of his own children."

Moreover, Clemens insists, over and over again, on the "storiness" of the novel. Its beginning, with the festive, ceremonial evocation of the bells ("surging and swelling"), which are then said to be "the Spirit of Storytelling," disarms the reader; the narrator, a pious kindly man, who is treated with both affection and irony, sustains this initial disarming throughout. He keeps warning us that what he has to tell is often "frightful" but he also always assures us that, in sum, it is "highly edifying." No fairy tale ever written has had more appeal and charm than *The Holy Sinner*.

But even if we should take *The Holy Sinner* seriously, attending to its meanings and fitting it into the Mann canon, we would probably still be constrained to say that the immediately preceding *Doctor Faustus*, deep and dark, is the true expression of our age and that the benign goodness of *The Holy Sinner* is false to our experience and is thus a "sport." In fact, the two books seem to constitute exactly and precisely truth and fancy, on all levels. *Doctor Faustus* is a massive book, *The Holy Sinner* is slight (perhaps on this ground alone to be dismissed); *Doctor Faustus* is a psychological and ideological account of modern man, *The Holy Sinner* is a pious and artless (seemingly) narration of a medieval legend; *Doctor Faustus* is, in its author's words, his "most savage" book, shaggy, grotesque, agonized—a massive galleon lurching through a storm-wracked darkness, with the eyes of heaven become the gates of hell. *The Holy Sinner* is neat, trim, geometrical—a shipshape little skiff sailing out of the night and darkness into a serene and clear dawn, over which a beneficent God presides.

Yet there are striking tie-ups between the two novels, so striking as to suggest that both novels are concerned with the same problems, albeit their respective answers are totally different. Both are narrated by Catholic humanists—*Doctor Faustus* by a teacher and *The Holy Sinner* by a monk. This means that a similar perspective—once agonized over the power of the Devil, once smiling over the mercy of God—prevails in both novels. Each novel is constructed upon the frame of a great Western myth (perhaps the two greatest) —Faust and the sin of pride, Gregory (Oedipus) and the sin of incest. Third, each of the novels is concerned with some aspect of medievalism: *The Holy Sinner* takes place in the Middle Ages, and *Doctor Faustus*, though of the present, is saturated, as its critics have remarked, with a certain kind of medievalism. Fourth and finally, it is the Gregory legend upon which Adrian Leverkühn constructs one of his compositions, and there is a narration and a discussion of the legend in *Doctor Faustus* itself. To this point I shall return in the conclusion, but first it will be necessary to describe the dialectical relationship of the assumptions underlying both novels.

In the world of *Doctor Faustus* everything from the physical universe to the human condition, mass and individual, is ambiguous. The universe itself has two chief characteristics: first, it is unlimited, or it appears to be so to human comprehension; and second, it lacks essential order since the boundaries between supposedly separate areas of activity constantly shift and merge. (Roughly, it is the universe given to the layman by modern science, although Mann attaches to this universe certain moral connotations which no scientist would probably allow.) This theme of equivocation is introduced at the beginning of the book by the very explicit symbol of Jonathan Leverkühn's desire to "speculate the elements." Thus he introduces the two boys, Adrian Leverkühn and Serenus Zeitblom, to a world that is distinguished chiefly by its ambiguities: areas overlap, limits are unknown, fantastic equivocations are the rule: butterflies whose beautiful colors are not really colors at all; ice flakes that "dabbled in the organic," a "devouring drop," "visible music," dead culture imitating organic form; and Zeitblom remarks:

> If I understood my host aright, then what occupied him was the essential unity of animate and so-called inanimate nature, it was thought that we sin against the latter when we draw too hard and fast a line between the two fields.

At all this equivocality Jonathan Leverkühn weeps; Zeitblom, the Catholic humanist, is uneasy; but Adrian, who is to make a pact with the Devil, laughs.

These original symbols are reinforced throughout the book in a variety of ways. In the dialogue between Leverkühn and the Devil, for example, there occurs a discussion of hell. *"Here everything leaves off"* is the most adequate descriptive metaphor that the Devil can contrive for human comprehension. And yet hell is something too, for, so Adrian is told, it is an alternation between the extremes of heat and cold (a condition which would constitute, in effect, a prolongation of Adrian's natural life). In short, hell is and is not. Again, in later life, Adrian has two intellectual hobbies: amateur studies of deep-sea life and of interstellar space. Besides the fact that the two areas are extremes, the attractions are obvious. In the deep sea Adrian finds a sphere of existence in which dwell "incredible eccentricities, some grisly, some comic, which nature here achieved, forms and features which seemed to have scarcely any connection with the upper world . . . frantic caricatures of organic life; predatory mouth opening and shutting; obscene jaws." To the ambiguities of these forms of life the apparent illimitability and disorder of what we call space is, for Adrian, a complementary interest:

> The physical universe . . . should be called neither finite nor infinite, because both words described something somehow static, whereas the true situation was through and through dynamic in its nature, and the cosmos, at least for a long time, more precisely for nineteen hundred million years, has been in a state of furious expansion — that is, of explosion.

But not only is the physical universe disordered and unmeasured; the same is true of the humans who inhabit it, and most of man's highest activities are shown to be questionable in nature. Music, which is one of the chief concerns in the book, is variously described as being highly equivocal in essence. Adrian first comes to it at the onset of puberty and at the time when he begins to suffer from migraine headaches. In other words, out of a conjunction of sex and pain issues a predilection for music. Zeitblom, the humanist student of literature, is suspicious of music and charges: "That intense but strangely inarticulate language, that of tones—if one may so designate music—does not seem to me to be included in the pedagogic-humanistic sphere." Adrian himself, playing chords on a piano, says: "Relationship is everything. And if you want to give it a more precise name, it is ambiguity." And his own music seems to exhibit the hellish tendencies of alternating between extremes of heat and cold. In the *Apocalypse* dissonance stands for the "lofty, solemn, pious, everything of the spirit," while consonance and firm tonality equal hell, the commonplace, and the banal. The chorus has been "instrumentalized" and the orchestra "vocalized." "Music," says Leverkühn early in the book, "turns the equivocal into a system."

Mathematics and theology, the two other chief intellectual interests of Leverkühn, are also shown to be "questionable" in character and position. "Mathesis," says Zeitblom, who was not adept at the science, "as applied logic, which yet confines itself to pure and lofty abstractions, holds a peculiar middle position between the humanistic and the practical sciences." Theology—in this case early twentieth-century Lutheranism—is likewise suspect. As carried on at Halle, where Leverkühn studies before turning to music, it is marked by brawling and controversy, and by subjective arbitrariness. Above all, as Zeitblom remarks here and elsewhere:

> Here one sees clearly the infiltration of theological thinking by irrational comments of philosophy, in whose realm, indeed, the non-theoretic, the vital, the will or instinct, in short the daemonic have long since become the chief theme of theory.

Zeitblom claims that religion without literature ("the humanistic science") inevitably tends toward the daemonic.

The implications of all this are summed up by Leverkühn himself, who says:

My Lutheranism . . . sees in theology and music neighboring spheres and close of kin; and besides, music has always seemed to me personally a magic marriage between theology and the so diverting mathematics.

Likewise is the social body in the world of *Doctor Faustus* invaded by the disordered, the irrational, the daemonic. Man's heritage from the past, in this case the medievalism that permeates the book, is lurid, sex-obsessed, witch-burning, fanatic. Of Kaisersaschern, Leverkühn's birthplace and always his spiritual home, Zeitblom remarks:

> But something still hung on the air from the spiritual constitution of the men of the last decades of the fifteenth century: a morbid excitement, a metaphysical epidemic latent since the last years of the Middle Ages. . . . Rash it may be to say so, but here one could imagine strange things: as for instance a movement for a children's crusade might break out; a St. Vitus's dance; some wandering lunatic with communistic visions, preaching a bonfire of the vanities; miracles of the Cross, fantastic and mystical folk-movements—things like these, one felt, might easily come to pass.

And the population of the town is remarkable for the number of grotesques it contains—a man of indefinite age who was given to executing a twitching dance in the streets, an old and witless woman who dressed, or tried to dress, like a French coquette, a man named Schnalle who added a senseless "Tootle-oo" to every statement he made.

If the heritage from the past is disordered, the present is even more so. Practically all the people with whom Leverkühn and Zeitblom come into contact lead futile, wasted lives and come to tragic ends: Clarissa Rodde commits suicide after her seducer threatens to expose her to her fiancé; Inez Institoris, indifferent to her superficial husband and a confirmed morphine addict, murders her lover, Rudi Schwerdtfeger, after his marriage to a woman whom he was supposedly courting for Leverkühn. And when World War I breaks out only Zeitblom, of all the men in their circle, goes into the army, for it is found that each of the other men has some fundamental physical defect.

The political-social body of which all these people are members is likewise disintegrative. During Leverkühn's sojourn at Halle the students are given to arguing politics. One of these debates, taking place out in the country where the young man are on a picnic, is particularly symbolic. No two debaters will agree, fantastic generalizations are thrown off, Naziism is shown in its incipiency. Finally they break off and fall asleep and Zeitblom comments:

> In reality it [the debate] had no end, it went on deep into the night, on and on, with "bipolar position" and "historically conscious analysis," with "extra-temporal qualities," "ontological naturalism," "logical dialectic," and "practical dialectic": painstaking, shoreless, learned, tailing off into nothing—

And since the time span of the book covers the period from 1885 to the 1940's, the Western world is steadily disintegrating under the impact of the two world wars. During the latter part of the book we are constantly reminded that Germany is about to be crushed by the Russians from the east and the Anglo-American forces from the west. At the very end, to the German narrator at least, literally everything seems to have been smashed, and the disintegration is total and overwhelming.

"I have learned in my philosophy courses," says Leverkühn to Zeitblom, "that to set limits already means to have passed them." Thus when we reach the heart of the matter, the individual human soul, we find the same limitlessness, disorder, and lack of measure that prevail in the universe, in the arts, and in society. Individualism is carried to its uttermost extreme, to the point where the tragic hero, Leverkühn, is utterly isolated and irrevocably damned. There is always a "coldness" about him, and he has no real relationship to anything human. His only genuine connections are symbolic and are either obscene

(the love affair with the mermaid) or evil (his intellec-
tual-artistic intercourse with the Devil). Syphilitic, mi-
graine-wracked, ridden by demons, he makes a pact with
the Devil, in order to produce great but despairing music.
His last great composition, *The Lamentation of Dr. Faustus,* was avowedly written to "take back" Beethoven's
Ninth Symphony. He is too proud to repent and, moreover, he believes, Calvinistically, that all was foreordained,
"man is made for hell or blessedness, made and foredes-
tined, and I was born for hell." Thus into the pitiless and
shifting infinity of evil of which the world is made, Leverkühn sinks and sinks: there is no God, no finiteness, no
foregiveness, nothing but limitless pain, limitless loneliness, limitless damnation, and, at the end, madness for
Leverkühn and total destruction for society.

The world of *The Holy Sinner* presents no such disordered extremes as does that of *Doctor Faustus.* It is more
of a piece, smaller, all compact, and further, an integrating
spirit pervades it, holding all together—the infinite mercy
of God. Only once is there a suggestion that there is a
realm of existence apart from this pervading spirit, and
this occurs when Clemens speculates on why nature would
allow such a monstrous thing as for a son to wed his own
mother.

> Why not? I desperately ask. He was a man and she was a
> woman and so they could become man and wife, for that is
> all that Nature cares about. My spirit cannot find itself in
> Nature; it rebels. She is of the Devil, for her indifference is
> bottomless . . . an indifference so bottomless that it is
> deeper than ignorance for it is her very self. Yes, Nature is
> all one, even to herself.

But then, with delightful irony, Mann turns Clemens
toward the comic by having him say (he has been talking
about the "wedding" night) "and supposing that Nature
had set her face against such ignorance, Grigorss would
have found himself in an awkward and unknightly situation; and this, again, I cannot wish for him." And he
continues: "In short they were very happy, not otherwise

can one express or report it, utterly and entirely happy."
So that finally human joy outweighs the potential fright-
fulness of nature, although, of course, this joy is inherently
sinful and must finally be renounced.

There is too in *The Holy Sinner* a suggestion of the
equivocal character of organic distinctions which form so
much of the substance of *Doctor Faustus*. When Gregory
is doing the seventeen years' penance on the stone, he
becomes greatly reduced in stature and all bristly; he
becomes, in short, or he appears to become, a "hedgehog":
man to animal. And the two Romans, who upon the
instructions of the bleeding lamb have come to seek him
out and crown him Pope, are horrified to find that Pope
Gregory to be is a "hedgehog." But again, this blurring of
lines is not allowed: "Do not take offence at my form!"
says Gregory to the Romans. "Nourishment for babes and
resistance to heaven's weathers have reduced it. Man's
estate will return to me." And so it is: normality reasserts
itself and within two hours, after eating bread and wine,
the "hedgehog" is metamorphosed into "a personable
man, of his age near forty, well-shapen, with long black
hair indeed, his face covered with a heavy growth of beard
which yet could not quite obscure the agreeableness of his
features."

This same idea of the inevitability of the reassertion of
the normal is likewise conveyed symbolically by Gregory's
finding of his tablet. This tablet, upon which was en-
graved the story of his incestuous birth, he had carried
with him for years, but he had left it behind when he
went to do the penance on the stone. The tablet had been
abandoned in a filthy shed which shortly after collapsed.
Now seventeen years later Gregory digs for it furiously.

> With the sleeves of his robe rolled up he thrust his billet
> now here, now there into the gore where once he had lain
> and with his own hands burrowed kneeling in the earth, so
> that one might say never did a man search with more fiery
> zeal for the charter and record of his sinful state. The
> nettles stung his hands but he paid no heed and God

rewarded the stings, the struggle, and the sweat, for lo, out of dung and mould it gleamed up at him and he drew out, clean and bright as though fresh from the framer's hand, even the ink undimmed.

Out of incest and "hedgehogs" come great Popes; out of dung and filth gleaming tablets: the reality, conversely from *Doctor Faustus*, is always more good, more true, and more beautiful than the appearance.

The concept of an over-all order in the world of *The Holy Sinner* is likewise suggested by the use of the number seventeen, for the time scheme of the novel is built upon a series of "seventeens": at the age of seventeen Wiligis and Sibylla, "the bad children," commit the original incestuous act; the fruit of this union, Gregory, is set adrift in a boat on the seventeenth day of his life; at about the same time his father dies, at the age of seventeen (*his* father had outlived his wife seventeen years); for seventeen years Gregory lives on an island and is brought up by monks; in his seventeenth year he returns to civilization, rescues his mother, now aged thirty-four, from a siege upon her city, and marries her. Then for three years they live in incest; discovering their crime, Gregory, now twenty, departs to do his penance which consists of staying on the rock for seventeen years; at the age of thirty-seven, he is released by the summons to become Pope and five years later he and his mother-wife have their final interview, this arranged by a seventeen-year-old boy whom Sibylla had sent to the Pope as her emissary. Nor is the choice of this particular number accidental, for according to Isidore Kozminsky's *Numbers: Their Meaning and Magic*, "seventeen" signifies as follows:

> In the *Sepher Yetzirah* the 17th Path is the Path of the Realization and Reward of the Righteous, for here is their Faith rewarded with the mantle of the Holy Spirit.

And this, of course, is what happens in *The Holy Sinner*: the man of faith ultimately rewarded by being made Pope. Above all the concept of the inevitable reassertion of the normal and the good and the concept of an over-all order are continually suggested by the presence of the all-merciful God. Clemens explains that he particularly chose this "tale at once frightful and highly edifying" because it illustrates so well "God's immeasurable and incalculable loving-kindness." So that the only limitlessness that exists in the universe lies not in the human sphere but in the spiritual, and there it is illustrated not by God's justice but by his mercy. "Man is finite," says Gregory, "Only God's mercy is infinite."

On the social and political level, order, normality, and limit also prevail. The outcome of a war is decided not by the total destruction of civilizations (although, to be sure, much damage has been done) but by single combat. A polyglot cosmopolitanism holds sway; so that the war cry of Gregory, when he is defending his "mother" against the warlike courtship of Roger the Goatbeard, is the Flemish or Franco-German "Niemalen de la vie!" As contrasted to the grotesques of *Doctor Faustus*, the characters here very often run to archetypes, general, typical norms. Maître Poitevin, the magistrate of the besieged city, is a classic Frenchman, consciously embodying the virtues which are legendarily attributed to the French.

"You are very shrewd, mine host," remarked Grigorss with respect.

"So am I," answered the other. "Would I otherwise have become Mayor of Bruges? Besides, my shrewdness takes the form of complete clarity and general intelligence."

Dame Eisengrein, who attends Sibylla during her pregnancy and at the birth of Gregory, is an archetypal woman-mother:

If he [Sieur Eisengrein] presented such an exceptionally firm and sturdy masculine picture, so she was feminine through and through, by nature and nurture, with her whole soul turned to feminine concerns—yes, except for God (she was very pious and wore a large jet cross on her mountainous bosom) she was interested in nothing at all but what has to do with women's life, in the most pious, most physical sense of the word.

And, finally, while civilization goes to smash at the end of *Doctor Faustus*, in *The Holy Sinner*, at the end, the schism in the Church over the two Popes is bound together by the "firm-holding" hand of Pope Gregory, and Western Christendom is joyously united under the beneficent saint. Fiercely stern with heresy—which is a profound threat to the essential order—tolerant and merciful toward the sins of the flesh—which constitute no genuine threat to faith—Gregory soon established a reputation as one who is more inclined to "loose" (forgive) than to "bind" (indict).

If the universe and society have limits and essential order, so too does the life of the individual, no matter how disordered it may at times appear to be. There is, for example, no such thing as complete human isolation. As Leverkühn was utterly separate from mankind, Gregory is, so to speak, overwhelmed with intimate familial-sexual ties. Son of his "uncle" and his "aunt," as Clemens calls them, he marries his mother-aunt and has by her two children whom he can only describe in his initial bewilderment upon finding out the truth as his aunt-mother-wife's "grandchildren." At the final interview he says to her: "A new task, dearest, have I set to your soul, but a merciful one: it is to grasp the three-in-oneness of child, spouse, and Pope." And at the last, in complete perplexity, they decide to become "brother" and "sister," once more, in a manner of speaking, only with different aims this time, and the children of their marriage are then Gregory's "nieces." As the Princess says: "Ah, Grigorss, the whole story is so beyond anything that the most astonishing thing in it astonishes no more." Thus, as Leverkühn is essentially "cold," one might say that Gregory is essentially "warm."

Nevertheless his relationships with his aunt-mother-wife are unqualifiedly sinful; he is mired in evil as much as Leverkühn. But infinity and limitlessness have no place in this world, nor does preordination. Things, no matter how bad, do come to an end. When the Princess gives way to despair, just before Gregory leaves, he admonishes her:

Lady, speak not thus, neither give way to despair, it is against the command. For of himself may man despair but not of God and His fullness of grace. We are both thrust into the marsh of sin up to our necks, and if you think you are deeper in, that is pridefulness. Add not this sin to the rest or the pool will go over mouth and nose.

So that while in *Doctor Faustus* no matter how bad things are they are bound to get worse, in *The Holy Sinner* no matter how bad things are they are bound to get better, as long as one does not give way to despair, the only unforgivable sin. For *The Holy Sinner* is saying, in contradistinction to *Doctor Faustus*, that the universe is finite; that there is a solid core of sanity and normality at the heart of human affairs, regardless of how grotesque and evil these affairs may at times appear to be; that moral evil is not unlimitedly regressive; and, finally, that there are no sins that cannot be forgiven, no tears that cannot be wiped away. And even at the end, when the Princess makes the ultimate admission of sin to the Pope, namely, that "conscious-unconscious" she suspected that she might be marrying her own son, he absolves her and adds, conjecturally, that there was a good possibility that the young Gregory had a suspicion that he was marrying his mother. But, despite all this, says Gregory in his last words in the book: "Everything has its limits—the world is finite."

There are also a number of other ways of expressing the nature of the dialectic between the two novels. Historically speaking, one might say, using the words not precisely but suggestively, that *Doctor Faustus* is Calvinistic and romantic; while *The Holy Sinner* is Catholic and classic. Or again that Mann has taken the two greatest of Western myths, has saturated each with a certain kind of medievalism, and has made one a profound tragedy, while with the other he gives a charming comic "answer" to the first. But the relationships, which are all differing aspects of the same central problem, are more precise than this; and at least three clues to them are contained in *Doctor Faustus* itself: one relating *The Holy Sinner* forward to the future of our art and culture, another relating *The Holy Sinner* back as a confrontation of *Doctor Faustus*, and a third relating this latest of his novels to Mann's work as a whole.

Mann apparently first came across the Gregory story while working on *Doctor Faustus*, for he has Leverkühn compose a suite based upon the *Gesta Romanorum*. The most striking part of the suite is concerned with "Of the Birth of the Holy Pope Gregory." In *Doctor Faustus* the whole story is related in detail and at some length and is characterized in such a way as to foreshadow uncannily the novel-to-be, *The Holy Sinner*. Zeitblom calls it, "this extravagantly sinful, simple, and appealing tale" and again: "The meeting of the Queen with the holy man whom she had borne to her brother, and whom she had embraced as spouse, charmed tears from us such as had never filled our eyes, uniquely mingled of laughter and fantastic sensibility." These two descriptions probably constitute the best short account yet written of the effect of *The Holy Sinner* upon the reader.

But it is upon Leverkühn himself that the tale has the greatest effect, for he sees in it a microcosmic adumbration of what art may be in the future, after humanity has made the new "break-through."

Isn't it amusing that music for a long time considered herself a means of release, whereas she herself, like all the arts, needed to be redeemed from pompous isolation, which was the fruit of the culture-emancipation, the elevation of culture as a substitute for religion—from being alone with an élite of culture, called the public, which soon will no longer be, which even now no longer is, so that soon art will be entirely alone, alone to die, unless she were to find her way to the folk, that is, to say it unromantically, to human beings? . . .

The whole temper of art, believe me, will change, and withal into the blither and more modest; it is inevitable, and it is a good thing. Much melancholy ambition will fall away from her, and a new innocence, yes, harmlessness will be hers . . . an art without anguish, psychologically healthy, not solemn, unsadly confiding, an art *per du* with humanity.

Even the humanist Zeitblom, who views with suspicion the "pompous isolation" and the "melancholy ambition" of Leverkühn's work, does not like this "folksy" prophecy. But it is the musician, Leverkühn, who has said it and it is the artist, Mann, who has written this work of the future in *The Holy Sinner*. Whatever one may think of the essential validity of Leverkühn's forecast, Mann, for himself, has brought it off, and has made of *The Holy Sinner* a wistful prophecy.

But *The Holy Sinner* has backward references as well, and once more *Doctor Faustus* contains the clue. In one sense, *The Holy Sinner* is a "taking back" of *Doctor Faustus*—that unrelievedly grim masterpiece—in the same sense that Leverkühn's *Lamentation of Dr. Faustus* "takes back" Beethoven's *Ninth*. Now of course there is, in the literal sense, no such thing as a cancellation of either *The Ninth Symphony* or *Doctor Faustus*. But if we say that human experience constitutes a 360° circle, then *Doctor Faustus* and the *Lamentation* are at one 180° pole and *The Ninth Symphony* and *The Holy Sinner* are at the other. The two pairs (and one of the four, of course, is only a metaphor) do not so much cancel out one another as they complement and expand one another. Only we are prevented from seeing their complementary character by the nature of our present situation. We seem to live exclusively in the world of *Doctor Faustus*, while the world of *The Holy Sinner* and of the music for Schiller's ode appears to be merely a pleasant dream.

For almost a century now in the literature of our civilization it has been assumed that the sane, the simple, the unqualifiedly good cannot be taken seriously; thus our inherent bent to equate simplicity to stupidity and complexity to intelligence; to give weight and value to the ambiguously evil and to place the simply good in an area beneath serious notice, if not contempt. Yet it must be remembered that an art which is not a substitute for religion, that is unpretentiously benign and humanistic, would have been perfectly meaningful to many past epochs and it may well happen that it will be perfectly meaningful to some in the future. By this I do not mean that other ages, past and future, have or will necessarily give assent to the religion, the Catholic, that is exemplified by *The Holy Sinner,* but that under the clear eye of man's larger history *The Holy Sinner* and what it stands for may prove to be a not contemptible antithesis to the thesis of such works as *Doctor Faustus.* It is, of course, extremely doubtful that anyone living today will ever share in a culture which, over against the ever-present powers of darkness, night, and death, will give serious weight and substantiality to the claims and powers of the simple, the sane, and the good, and which will be in a position to allow the hope of heaven to hold its own against the powers of hell. For we have lost, for the present anyway, the power to understand or to take seriously the simple and the benign. And while man at his most highly conscious and quintessential moments may always be more a suffering member of the *Doctor Faustus* world than anything else, still *The Holy Sinner* reminds us that *Doctor Faustus* is the product of an extreme cultural situation and that the essential and long-term human condition lies, sphinx-like and wavering, between these two extremes of utter damnation and utter benignity.

There remains finally the question of where *The Holy Sinner* exists in relation to all the rest of Mann's work. Here again he is his own best commentator and once again the directional hint comes from *Doctor Faustus.* In lecturing on Beethoven's Sonata, Op. 121, Wendell Kretschmar says:

> The characteristic of the movement of course is the wide gap between bass and treble, between the right and the left hand, and a moment comes, an utterly extreme situation, when the poor little motif seems to hover alone and forsaken above a giddy yawning abyss—a procedure of awe-inspiring unearthliness, to which then succeeds a distrustful making-of-itself-small, a start of fear as it were, that such a

thing could happen. Much else happens before the end. But when it ends and while it ends, something comes, after so much rage, persistence, obstinacy, extravagance: *something entirely unexpected and touching in its mildness and goodness* . . . [Italics mine]. It is like having one's hair or cheek stroked, lovingly, understandingly, like a deep and silent farewell look. It blesses the object, the frightfully harried formulation, with overpowering humanity, lies in parting so gently on the hearer's heart in eternal farewell that the eyes run over.

In an interview published in the *New York Times Book Review* in June 1951, Mann announced that after *The Holy Sinner* he would write no more "deep" books—for the present anyway—but would revert to his early naturalism and picture streams of events rather than streams of thought. This is only fitting and just, since he has said everything "deep" that he has to say—for the present, once more—and has rounded off the "deep" period by writing its conclusion, for *The Holy Sinner* is the coda, "entirely unexpected and touching in its mildness and goodness," to all the work that has gone before and especially to the "giddy yawning abyss" of *Doctor Faustus*: *The Magic Mountain,* anatomy of the present; *Joseph and His Brothers,* descent into the past; *Doctor Faustus,* descent into hell; *The Holy Sinner,* emergence, benediction, blessing. Like Chaucer and so many of the medieval writers, Mann has in a sense written a retraction, which is essentially an assertion of faith. For *The Holy Sinner* is a book surpassingly and piercingly sweet: it is a prayer, and an act of forgiveness—for its author and for us all.

IT IS A TRUISM that both the form and the content of the novel are bound up, more than is the case in any other of the major literary forms, with the dialectic between man and time and / or history. Upon this primordial fulcrum, which leans, in one direction, toward the private, the individual, the subjective and, in another and opposite direction, toward the public, the collective, the objective, the novel rests, achieving grandeur, like all art, only insofar as it maintains an equivocal synthesis, constantly breaking down and knitting together, between these two diametrically different but interacting areas of human experience. "Thus," writes Santayana, "two concomitant yet strangely different streams would seem to compose human life: one the vast cosmic flood of cyclic movements and sudden precipitations, in which man has his part like other animals; and the other, the private little rivulet of images, emotions, and words babbling as we move, and often hidden underground in sleep or forgetfulness." Santayana's aphorism, which sounds like a capsule-description of *Finnegans Wake,* is saying, like *Finnegans Wake,* that human experience is simultaneously a public nightmare and a private dream. And it is precisely this perspectivist observation post over the life of man that the great novelists have commanded, from Cervantes to Joyce. But the exact artistic formulation differs from author to author, and, more importantly, from century to century.

"A nous deux maintenant," says Rastignac (the private

dream) to Paris (the public nightmare). This is the classic nineteenth-century formulation of the dialectic between man and time-history: the individual (here conceived of not as a psychic unit but as a whole, socio-biological person) clashing and coalescing with the city (contemporary history). But the twentieth-century purview of Stephen Dedalus includes not only the city and contemporary history but the nightmare of universal time-history as well. So that the major movement in the novel over the last one hundred years consists of a successive radicalizing of the two sides of the antithesis, with the individual becoming more and more a purely psychic entity, finally turning into a literal private dream, and time-history becoming more and more all-embracing until it eventually becomes a literal, public, multi-encompassing nightmare. *Finnegans Wake* formulates the dialectic in terms at once the most minute and grandiose: the ego dreaming on the history of the universe. The basic categories in the two centuries remain the same, but, whereas the nineteenth-century novel filled them out normatively, prosaically, the twentieth-century novel fills them out violently, grotesquely.

It is the purpose of this essay to trace out the broad outlines, using for illustrative material the history of the British novel of the last one hundred years, of this movement from man-social history to ego-universal history, in terms of the differing conceptions of and differing metaphors for the idea of time-history, with final remarks concerning, first, the bearings of these metaphors upon the conventions symbolizing personality and, secondly, the relationships between the idea of man and the idea of time-history.

The Platonic tradition held that time was "the moving image of eternity." This definition, while it may well be philosophically unsound, is just artistically and imaginatively if we grant that Everyman must somehow come to terms with time-history and evolve for it an emotionally satisfying metaphor which then constitutes an emblem of things ultimate. This is one of the things that literature attempts to do. But if we say that the time-sense and the historical-sense of a work of art is "the moving image of eternity" and is, as Spengler and others have held, profoundly axiological, we must still have more precise categories for more specific analysis. The categories most often used, of course, are the time-space antitheses. Yet to hypostasize time as a discrete entity is to pass over precedent aspects of the problem, for there are, in life and art and anterior to the space-time antithesis, several divergent metaphors for describing time-history itself.

According to the late Nicholas Berdyaev there are three basic categories and symbols for describing time-history (Berdyaev makes no distinction between the time-sense and the historical-sense, taking them both to be specific manifestations of the general attitude toward temporal experience). First, there is cosmic time, which can be symbolized by a circle and which refers to the endless recurrence of things: night following day, season following season, the cycle of birth, growth, and decay; in short the circular character of human and natural experience. Secondly, there is historical time, symbolized by a horizontal line, and referring to the course of nations, civilizations, tribes (i.e., mankind in the mass) through time. Likewise the individual has a linear as well as a circular relationship to time. The line, for man or men, may slant upward, to indicate progress, or downward, to indicate regress. Third, and symbolized by a vertical line, there is existential time, referring to a notion of time somewhat like Bergson's *durée*, only religious or mystical in nature. This concept of existential time is actually an extreme form of individualism, or in Berdyaev's words, "personalism," and presupposes the individual's ability to free himself from either cyclic or historical time. Existential time, in effect, denies the validity of time-history. Historically, this idea of time manifested itself in the apocalyptic tendencies of early Christianity; in secular terms it still survives in certain anarchist doctrines. Popularly, it receives prosaic expression in the old wives' tale about a drowning man's whole life flashing before him in an instant, and, generally, in the common notion that, in all men's psychological experience, time has differing speeds and, at certain critical moments, seems, almost, to stop.

The time-sense of the Victorians was, of course, the linear one, which for twentieth-century man, so accustomed to the idea of "recurrence," seems to be almost equivalent to having no time-sense at all. In fact what appears, for us, to be absent in most Victorian novels — this despite the preoccupation of the nineteenth century with the past — is precisely an acute sense of time and a deep sense of history. And we do not need to go all the way up to Joyce, Proust, and Mann to see the difference between the central Victorians and us in these matters. Hardy and James will do.

In the work of neither Dickens nor Trollope, to take them as our examples, is there any of what one might call "metaphysical" concern with time. Both authors, of course, were signally unintellectual and uninterested in such matters. They did use time for a certain shock value, for it was "in time" that the convolutions of plot were unravelled, the hero restored, and so on. But their time convention was vague and loose as compared, for example, to the rigorously observed "continuous present" of the late James. Trollope was given to suspending novel time altogether, by dropping the narrative and candidly predicting future events. In *The Eustace Diamonds* the diamonds at one point mysteriously disappear, as far as most of the characters in the novel are concerned, but Trollope informs the reader thus:

> In the mean time, the Eustace diamonds were locked up in a small safe fixed into the wall at the back of a small cellar beneath the establishment of Messrs. Harter and Benjamin, in Minto Lane, in the City. Messrs. Harter and Benjamin always kept a second place of business. Their great shop was at the West End; but they had accommodations in the city.
>
> The chronicler states this at once, as he scorns to keep from his reader any secret that is known to himself.

In other words novel time to Trollope was a joke. Generally he assumed that a convention of time existed and that the essence of his art, along with delineation of character, was temporality and that only by the passage of time would events unfold. But Trollope, like the rest of the Victorians, practiced a narrative method which explicitly allowed the author to see before and after, and hence for him as for God, there was no time and eternity lay spread before him. Thus every so often, banteringly (and Thackeray did the same thing), Trollope told the reader that novel time was his, and the reader's, sport, to be suspended at will, as the novelist desires. With how little seriousness novel time was taken by Trollope and the other Victorians can best be realized by comparing the above novelistic convention, which is not at all uncharacteristic of the Victorians, with the intricate "time-shift" of Ford and Conrad, where time is a cross to bear.

What is also absent in both Trollope and Dickens, and in most of the other Victorians, George Eliot perhaps excepted, particularly in the Jewish passages of *Daniel Deronda,* is a powerful sense of history. Of course practically all of the Victorians, following Scott, wrote historical novels, and, as a rule, failed to recapture and reconstruct a valid representation of the age they were concerned with. Yet their lack of historical sense is not best exemplified by these partial failures, although one might say that they were bound to fail, given their general attitude toward human history. What is absent in the Victorians is that more profound sense of the past (deeper than any fascination for the past as picturesque or the past as more attractive socially, in the fashion that Thackeray was intrigued by the eighteenth century) — the obsession of modern man that the past is continually impinging on the present and assuming the proportions of a nightmare.

The classic Victorian attitude toward history and the attitude which underlay most of its literary conventions is presented most unequivocally by Dickens, whose opinion of his collective heritage was negative, to say the least. Dickens had only pity and contempt for those unfortunates who had been born at other times and in other places than nineteenth-century England (although this is not to imply that he thought that he himself was living in paradise). It is reported that he had, in his library at Gadshill, a set of false backs which purported to be a history of Western civilization and which bore the following general and specific titles: "The Wisdom of our Ancestors—I. Ignorance. II. Superstition. III. The Block. IV. The Stake. V. The Rack. VI. Dirt. VII. Disease." So much for the past.

Turning now to James and Hardy, one finds quite a different situation. Both James and Hardy, in different ways, represent the ingress of temporal and historical preoccupations in the British novel. James was one of the first novelists to take time seriously and to make it an implicit part of his work. Preeminently in James things happen in time. In the typical James novel, meaning a late novel, all the psychic action is seen as the relentless unfolding of time, minute by minute, hour by hour, year by year, within the mind or sensibility of an individual.

History or the sense of the past likewise begins to appear in the novels of James. James, of course, did not have the historical imagination of his friend Henry Adams with its conception of man's past as a construct of great forces bearing down on the present. Nevertheless, it is history that plays, generally, a major role in the motivation of all James's novels and it is history that became an obsessional preoccupation in his late works. In James's abiding theme—the American in Europe—the sense of the past is one of Europe's most subtle blandishments, something that pierces the soul and makes one laugh and weep simultaneously. Thus Isabel Archer on seeing the Eternal City for the first time:

> She had always been fond of history, and here was history in the stones of the street and the atoms of sunshine. She had an imagination that kindled at the mention of great deeds, and wherever she turned some great deed had been acted. These things strongly moved her, but moved her all inwardly. . . . By her own measure she was very happy; she would even have been willing to take these hours for the happiest she was ever to know. The sense of the terrible human past was heavy to her, but that of

something altogether contemporary would suddenly give it wings that it could wave in the blue. Her consciousness was so mixed that she scarcely knew where the different parts of it would lead her, and she went about in a repressed ecstasy of contemplation, seeing often in the things she looked at a great deal more than was there, and yet not seeing many of the items enumerated in her Murray.

This sense of the past became successively more acute in James's works and is the explicit and sole concern in some of the late tales and novels. In *The Altar of the Dead* the protagonist perpetually lights candles in commemoration of the dead, or the past; the hero of *The Jolly Corner* symbolically recaptures his own past; and, most bizarrely, Ralph Pendrel of the late unfinished novel *The Sense of the Past* actually changes place with a dead ancestor. And here, in this novel, James gave his most magniloquent testimony to the force of human history:

> On the day he disembarked in England he felt himself as never before ranged in that interest [the past], counted on that side of the line. It was to this he had been brought by his desire to remount the stream of time, really to bathe in its upper and more natural waters, to risk even, as he might say, drinking of them. No man, he well believed, could ever so much have wanted to look behind and still behind—to scale the high wall into which the successive years, each a squared block, pile themselves in our rear and look over as nearly as possible with eye of sense into, unless it should be called out of, the vast prison house. . . . If his idea in fine was to recover the lost moment, to feel the stopped pulse, it was to do so as experience, in order to be again consciously that creature that had been, to breathe as he had breathed and feel the pressure he had felt.

In Hardy too time is taken seriously and becomes, in fact, dramatized as a malignant Fate, lying ominously in the future, waiting to strike down humans. Likewise everything in Hardy, natural or human, reverberates with history. The background for Hardy's Wessex series is provided by an immemorial community, the peasantry, who are, in a literal sense, the past, and who surround the main characters with an aura of ancient custom, legend, and myth, and the landscape itself mutely speaks for and of the ages.

But if time and history had become more pressing and more of a concern in the later nineteenth-century novel, they had also become something quite different, in their very nature; and a new set of literary conventions arose to symbolize the new attitudes. Dickens and Trollope were committed, by their unconscious assumptions and by the literary conventions which they inherited, to historical time, or time as a straight line, from the past into the future. In their case the idea of time was tied up with the idea of progress; so that the line of history led upward and receded downward, with the result that one looked forward to a pleasant but indefinite future and shunned a definite but unpleasant past. This attitude—rationalistic, progressive, secular—is, of course, the heritage of the eighteenth century and is known as liberalism. But what is noteworthy about the liberal attitude toward time-history is that, while it is generally confident about the future, it is vague about the concrete content of the future, as compared, say, to a Marxist, a conservative, or a cyclist. The key here is the ending of a novel, which is a specific and concrete manifestation of the general sense of time-history underlying the novel as a whole. At the end of a Dickens novel, for example, the leading characters are briefly projected into the future. But as George Orwell said, although the reader is assured of the infinite happiness of all parties, he is never quite sure as to why they are happy or what they are happy at, save that there is a childbirth every year and a Christmas spirit all the time. The assumption about futurity here is that these happy few will continuously but mistily compound their happiness, piling cheer on cheer, for the rest of their mortality. In short, the Victorian convention of the "happy ending" was not simply the result of a solid society wishing to have its sense of the fitness of things reaffirmed, for there is plenty of evidence to prove that the Victorian was anything but the stable and unworried cultural group that it is often supposed to have been. The "happy ending" does make sense if it be regarded as a literary convention metaphorically expressing the Victorian time-sense; i.e., man projected into an imprecise but, nevertheless, happy future. And for the Victorian novelist, before the "happy ending" happened, the substance of things and the material for his novel was a reality composed of an historically-emptied conjunction of the present and the future.

With Hardy and James it is precisely this concept of time and history as a straight line, leading upward, that begins to break down. Hardy's sense of the past is, partially anyway, a metaphorical expression of cosmic time, whose essence is the endless recurrence of things. In *The Return of the Native* an entire cycle of nature takes place, while the humanity in the foreground works itself out into an unhappy and ambiguous ending. Likewise in so many of the other Wessex novels, the one immutable certainty is that nature will continue her ceaseless cycle, no matter what sad fate besets man. As in nature so in man: the only solidity that man possesses is that which he inherits from the past, and Hardy's natives, like Faulkner's negroes, "endure." For the moderns, the civilized, the rationalists, the dependents on a liberalist future, the type who in the Victorian novel had the "happy ending," there is only tragedy, or misery, waiting in the future. In other words the universe of Thomas Hardy has only one certitude, the cyclic character of existence, and only one prop for humans, an allegiance to the past.

James's time-sense was obviously different from Hardy's and is, in effect, a secular version of existential or subjective time. Ralph Pendrel of *The Sense of the Past* literally fulfills Berdyaev's definition of existential time—he escapes from history. Less obvious is the implicit sense of existential time in all of James's late work, where there is no objective reality, and thus no real time, outside of the mind of the individual. Moreover, this internal time, while it flows continuously, does not always move at a constant rate. What happens in James is that time is extricated from history, as, with the clock stopped, James explores, often for pages, the infinity of implications arising from an instantaneous impression, and, in a sense, James's late works constitute a long essay on the potential infinity of individual psychological moments.

As in the case of the Victorians, the key to Hardy's and James's time-sense is the manner in which each ends his novels. They both wrote "happy endings" but their most characteristic novels end either tragically (Hardy) or ambiguously (James). This is to say that man's future is either dark or unsure. In Hardy and in James, then, simple historical time, built along the idea of progress, is breaking down and cosmic and existential time are becoming the province of the novelist, who is, simultaneously, developing an historical sense and an immortal desire for an immersion in the past. It should be added that with James, at least, the novel is turning away from the objective world of society toward the inner world of the self for its subject matter.

Of Joyce's preoccupation with time-history, nothing need be said. He had, said Wyndham Lewis in paying the highest insult he could think of, a "time-mind." Nor do I propose to unravel the incredibly elaborate time-history structures underlying *Ulysses* and *Finnegans Wake*. For the purpose of this essay, however, *Ulysses* and *Finnegans Wake* may be taken as the uttermost extensions of the movements in the British novel being sketched here. As compared to Hardy, where a cosmic vision of time-history appeared only in regard to nature, the cycles in Joyce are all-inclusive, embracing human experience in its entirety, from personal, to social and natural, to, finally, divine history. As compared to James, where a limited existentialist time is employed at certain times, in Joyce the moment actually becomes infinity. "I hear," thinks Stephen Dedalus, "the ruin of all space, shattered glass and toppling masonry, and time one livid final flame." Thus in *Finnegans Wake* every moment is infinity and everything in history happens in every moment. Existential and cosmic time here coincide, producing a continuous, multileveled present which, by the principle of infinite regress, constantly recapitulates the key events of human and divine history, preeminently the Fall of Man. This concept of time-history could be symbolized in Berdyaev's categories as follows: time-history is a series of concentric circles; at dead center is H.C.E. (Man) who rays out vertical lines of existential being in all directions and through all levels of the cyclic experiences. Joyce has made incommensurables—the circular and the vertical—complement one another.

Likewise the implication for human destiny of the endings of *Ulysses* and *Finnegans Wake* is neither the vague happiness of the Victorians nor the ambiguous tragedy of James and Hardy. Joyce had the concrete circular vision—everything that has happened before will happen all over again—and it is this assumption that makes Joyce's work the true "tower beyond tragedy." At the end of *Ulysses* we know that Bloom will arise the next day and, with slight and unessential differences, will repeat his day-cycle once more. At the end of *Finnegans Wake* the cycle is made even more explicit by the famous broken sentence whose end can be found at the beginning of the book.

At this point the novel has turned from its Victorian standing-ground at a conjunction of the present-future to a conjunction of the past-present; and time-history, formerly a prosaic segment in the life of the city, in the linear image, has become a giant nimbus of exfoliating circles, shot through with existential lines of being.

While the concept and metaphor for time-history were expanded and elaborated, the concept and metaphor for characterology contracted and intensified. Thus Dickens' eccentrics with their diamond-hard outlines turned, finally, into Joyce's blurred and fluxial egos, with their shadowy archetypal bases. In both the line of expansion and contraction, James's late novels appear to be a critical stage, for here the novel, in matters of character, is narrowing down, simultaneously decreasing the number in the cast of characters and turning away from the world

into the self; at the same time there is an elaborate bur-
geoning of the idea of time-history into a complex metaphor which affords a glimpse of eternity and provides a
bizarre vision of life, under which man, now time-
obsessed, is, at certain moments, free of time and, at other
moments, bears the whole of human history, like a cross,
upon his back.

And the case of James points out too the intimate
interconnection between these two lines of contraction
and expansion, in fact, their cause-and-effect relationship.
James's methods and interests led straight to the central
convention of the early twentieth-century novel, that is,
"the stream of consciousness" or "interior monologue."
And this device, while its most obvious function was to
body forth the inner life in a fashion impossible within
the nineteenth-century novelistic conventions, was also a
way of objectifying time-history in a manner unavailable
to the Victorians: first it permitted the illusion of a continuous present (the existential), and, second, it permitted by reverie and memory, exploration of the past and
the juxtaposition and confounding of past with present
(the cosmic). It is only one more step for the individual
memory, with which the "stream of consciousness" was
initially concerned, to step over into collective memory
and thus pass out into history.

Historically this is about what happened, for as the
novel turned inward and contemporary history became
thinned and abstracted (the late as opposed to the early
James, for example), universal history began to emerge. In
Thomas Mann's words, "the bourgeois and individual
passes over into the mythical and typical." As in the
children's fable, one digs a hole in the ground, to turn
away from the world, but finally emerges in China, and, as
a matter of fact, when one thinks of James's famous
pagoda and caravan images or the orientalism of *Finnegans Wake*, the analogy is apt.

What has happened, then, in the novel is that the two
sides of the basic antithesis of the novel (the private
dream and the public nightmare) have had their respec-

tive time-schemes changed. Whereas both once traveled the linear line of historical time, in the twentieth-century novel the individual's time-sense has been, in great part, existentialized and the time-scheme of the universe has been circularized. *Finnegans Wake* carries these twin, complementary movements to their highest and most equivocal pitch, into an area, in fact, where they are breaking down, one into the other, and where the parallels of development are beginning to curve and cross: a subjectivity, on the side of the individual, so complete, minute, and intense that it is constantly verging into the most broad and representative kind of archetypism; a vision of time-history so elaborate, so all-encompassing, so grandiose that it threatens, continually, to turn into a private, esoteric, mystagogic poem. Yet *Finnegans Wake* achieves the balance between the private and the public, the "perspectivism" which the great novel, since *Don Quixote*, has always achieved, albeit here in a radical, almost desperate fashion. And the success of this equivocal equation is, in great part, due to the organic blend of two kinds of time: the existential being the most extreme form of individualism; the cosmic being the most impersonal and objective way of describing the incessant tick, whose meaning is a circle, that sounds throughout *Finnegans Wake* and in all our ears.

4 FITZGERALD'S
THE GREAT GATSBY
LEGENDARY BASES AND
ALLEGORICAL SIGNIFICANCES

THE GREAT GATSBY is not merely concerned with the American twenties—it is a novel about American history as a whole, about Europe, and about eternity. For underlying this seemingly slight novel are all the great legends, with their allegorical significances, that American history has generated: the legend of New York City; the legend of the East versus the West; the legend of the North versus the South; the legend of America versus Europe; and behind them all is a compelling description of the human condition, irrespective of time and place.

The city of New York, to take the first legend first, is not really a part of the United States at all. It is therefore, in *The Great Gatsby*, enchanted ground, and the thunderous moral artillery that Fitzgerald brings to bear upon the rest of America and, by implication, on Europe simply does not here apply. New York rouses only the faculty of wonder and delight; it is beyond judgment; indeed, it is beyond good and evil.

" 'Anything can happen now that we've slid over the bridge . . . anything at all . . .' " thinks Nick Carraway to himself as he drives over the Queensborough Bridge in Gatsby's limousine. Gatsby himself has just demonstrated that the usual rules do not apply by flashing a white card in the face of a policeman who had intended to stop them for speeding but who, after seeing the card, tips his hat respectfully and says, " 'Know you next time, Mr. Gatsby. Excuse *me!* ' " And Fitzgerald with his gift for rich but compact social documentation immediately provides two images that spell out, metaphorically, the fact that *the* City is not a part of the ordinary world. One is the image of death, of a hearse and a funeral procession of automobiles in the windows of which appear "the tragic eyes and the short upper lips of southeastern Europe." In this pictorial juxtaposition of the funeral of an immigrant from Southeastern Europe and the speeding splendid limousine of the young American with the specious Oxford accent and the mysterious past and present, Fitzgerald suggests all the bizarre economic, social, and racial nonsequiturs that the enchanted city contains. The second image is one of life and is more simple and concrete. For the next sight, after the funeral procession, is "a limousine . . . driven by a white chauffeur, in which sat three modish Negroes, two bucks and a girl . . . the yolks of their eyeballs rolled toward us in haughty rivalry."

This last image might suggest that New York still possessed all the old stresses and strains of the rest of the country, only in reversed form. But such is not the case at all, for once inside the city, one is in an atmosphere that can suggest, in Fitzgerald's words, the "pastoral." Thus he says of Fifth Avenue on a quiet afternoon:

> We drove over to Fifth Avenue, warm and soft, almost pastoral, on the summer Sunday afternoon. I wouldn't have been surprised to see a great flock of white sheep turn the corner.

Behind Fitzgerald's special legend of New York as "pastoral" lies the traditional American idea of New York as the city of wonder and mystery and man-made magnificence, through which the sensitive young man wanders alone, experiencing vicariously beauty and power. As in Thomas Wolfe's massive reveries, the experienced woman with the enigmatic smile is the central symbol. If in the hinterlands a young man wants a "girl friend," on Manhattan Island he wants a woman. And Fitzgerald gives a few paragraphs to the theme that Wolfe had dilated volume by volume:

> I began to like New York, the racy, adventurous feel of it at night . . . I liked to walk up Fifth Avenue and pick out romantic women from the crowd and imagine that in a few minutes I was going to enter their lives and no one would ever know or disapprove . . . At the enchanged metropolitan twilight I felt a haunting loneliness, and felt it in others.

The action of the novel shuttles back and forth between this bizarre but enchanted metropolis, and the bizarre but corrupt Eggs, East and West, on Long Island. And while the class lines are strictly observed in the Eggs, in New York a wild democracy prevails. Thus it is in New York that the staunch defender of Teutonic purity and the conservative philosopher for the class society, Tom Buchanan, introduces Nick Carraway to his mindless, smouldering paramour, Myrtle Wilson, and to their New York "Social circle": Catherine, Myrtle's sister, freshly back from Monte Carlo by way of Marseilles—"God, how I hated that town"; pale, feminine Mr. McKee, the photographer from the flat below, in the "artistic game," as he calls it; and the toady Mrs. McKee. As the shabby bacchanal reaches its climax there is the little mongrel dog "sitting on the table looking with blind eyes through the smoke, and from time to time groaning faintly," the two empty bottles of whiskey, and finally "the short deft movement" of Tom Buchanan's hand as he breaks the nose of Myrtle.

It is in New York too that Nick meets the incredible Mr. Wolfsheim, the man who fixed the World Series. Wolfsheim has his offices for his official business, called the "Swastika Holding Company"; he eats luncheon at mid-town restaurants, just like any respectable businessman, but it is a business based on bootleg liquor and shady securities, and it can involve sudden death. Wolfsheim, as it turns out, is the only native-born New Yorker—in fact the only native-born Easterner—who plays a major role in the novel. It is indicative of Fitzgerald's attitude toward New York and toward "respectable" wealth that Wolfsheim should be one of the most decent characters in the book, infinitely superior to those who have "honestly" inherited "honest" money. Although he refuses, by reason of his peculiar business activities, to attend Gatsby's funeral (he would certainly have done so in his younger days, he explains to Nick), he is finally the author of one of the most humane pronouncements in the book, as he passes his final benediction on his dead protégé: " 'Let us learn to show our friendship for a man when he is alive and not after he is dead. After that, my own rule is to let everything alone.' "

Finally, New York is the setting for that uncourtly joust between Tom and Gatsby for the body and soul of Daisy. As if by instinct, the characters agree to repair to New York for this strange dénouement, where on a hot afternoon in the suite of a New York hotel and to the muffled music of Mendelssohn emanating from the ballroom below, where a marriage is taking place, Gatsby's dream shatters itself against the hard malice of Tom Buchanan and the "slydinge of corage" of Daisy.

But if New York is an enchanted place, where none of the ordinary mores and morals obtain and where gangsters are benign, it is surrounded by a rich corruption — what Nick Carraway calls the "East" — whose microcosmic symbols are West and East Egg, and whose antithesis is Nick's "Middle West." This opposition between the Eastern United States and the Middle Western is one of the major legends of the novel and is Nick Carraway's story, which blends into and complements the legend of America as a whole, which is the story of Gatsby. But Gatsby's life and his imperishable vision are so overwhelmingly romantic and so endlessly suggestive and so terribly pathetic that they get all the attention from most readers to the exclusion of one half of the book, which is the mind and times of Nick Carraway, whose framing intelligence binds the novel together and whose articulate moral sense evaluates a good deal of its meaning.

At first glance the East-West legend seems to be the traditional one of urban, corrupt East as opposed to bucolic, innocent West. While this immemorial antithesis is certainly in the background, Fitzgerald, as with New York, considerably modifies and complicates the original metaphor. In the first place, the three chief male characters, each radically different, are all Midwesterners, and the most corrupt person in the book, Tom Buchanan, is from Chicago; Gatsby himself, partly corrupted by his partly corrupted dream, in whose wake swirls "foul dust," is from North Dakota. Only Nick, from an unspecified town of "wide lawns and friendly trees," in an unspecified state (probably Minnesota), manages to hold fast, morally speaking. These facts are further complicated, at the conclusion of the novel, by Nick's assertion that all the major characters are "Westerners," and brooding over their diverse fates he thinks:

> I see now that this has been a story of the West, after all—Tom and Gatsby, Daisy and Jordan and I, were all Westerners, and perhaps we possessed some deficiency in common which made us subtly unadaptable to Eastern life.

This assertion is true in the sense that all of these characters were born and reared west of New York, but it is an oversimplification of the novel itself. For Jordan Baker and Daisy Fay are unmistakably from the South, a fact which introduces another legend altogether, and Tom, and his home town, Chicago, are unmistakably in a fallen condition in the first place. In this one sentence Fitzgerald did express the traditional East-West antithesis, but the facts presented in the novel as a whole considerably qualify this simple pattern.

While there is one East in the novel, there are several Wests, the most important of which is a certain part of the Middle West. The Far West, so called, is only briefly suggested and in three ways—two relating to the nineteenth century and one to the twentieth. As for the past, first, the empire-builder, robber-baron legend is evoked by poor old James Gatz, who, coming on from Minnesota after his son's death and excited by the tangible evidences of splendor in Gatsby's grotesque mansion, exclaims: "If he'd of lived, he'd of been a great man. A man like James J. Hill. He'd of helped build up the country." Another and wilder West of the past is given fuller embodiment in the sketch of the life and times of Dan Cody, Montana copper millionaire and Gatsby's first tutor and employer.

If the evocation of the real and notorious James J. Hill is pathetic, the picture of this fictional "empire-builder," Cody, is unsavory—"a gray, florid man with a hard empty face—the pioneer debauchee, who during one phase of American life brought back to the Eastern seaboard the savage violence of the frontier brothel and saloon." It would seem, then, that Fitzgerald's West is not that of the entrepreneur.

The modern Far West gets into the novel in two ways: first, as a place—Tom and Daisy return from their South Seas honeymoon to stay in Santa Barbara, and it is through an automobile accident on the Ventura Road that Tom's first infidelity is revealed—and, second, as a twentieth-century symbol of unreality. This last, of course, is Hollywood, and at one of Gatsby's parties Daisy is entranced by a glimpse of a movie star, "a gorgeous, scarcely human orchid of a woman who sat under a white-plum tree." A piratical railroad builder, a debauched miner, a nonhuman orchid sitting under a white-plum tree in pale moonlight is all that the far West can conjure up.[1]

The moral center, then, of *The Great Gatsby* lies somewhere in the Middle West, but there are more qualifications to be made about this region. Chicago, for example, is as corrupt as the East. When Tom and Daisy return from France, they settle first in Tom's original home town, Jordan Baker tells Nick, where "They moved with a fast crowd all of them young and rich and wild." Jordan goes on to speculate about Daisy's chastity at this time in her life and finally impugns it: "Perhaps Daisy never went in for amour at all—and yet there's something in that voice of hers."

Virtue then is not to be found or cultivated here, but neither is it radically potential on the Middle-Western farm, at least not on the farm of the "shiftless and unsuccessful" James Gatz. It lies in the home town and in the lineage and upbringing of Nick Carraway. Geographically, Nick's home is west of Chicago. Reminiscing about his prep school and college days, Nick remembers that he felt that he was getting into home territory only after the train had left Chicago:

> When we pulled out into the winter night and the real snow, our snow, began to stretch out beside us and twinkle against the windows, and the dim lights of small Wisconsin stations moved by, a sharp wild brace came suddenly into the air. We drew in deep breaths of it as we walked back from the diner through the cold vestibule, unutterably aware of our identity with this country for one strange hour, before we melted indistinguishably into it again.

> That's my Middle West.

The moral center of the universe, then, lies somewhere west of Chicago but east of what could be called the Far West. But it is not rural; it is urban, although not metropolitan and, more importantly, it is traditional, conservative, and house-centered. In Nick's words,

> not the wheat or the prairies or the lost Swede towns, but the thrilling returning trains of my youth, and the street lamp and sleigh bells in the frosty dark and the shadows of holly wreaths thrown by lighted windows on the snow. I am part of that, a little solemn with the feel of those long winters, a little complacent from growing up in the Carraway house in a city where dwellings are still called through decades by a family's name.

What Fitzgerald has done here is to add the idea of class to the idea of place. The kind of class that he attributes to Nick Carraway's family suggests that of the one great American cultural component that had its origin in the major region that he never expressly mentions in the novel—namely New England, with its ideal of a comfortable, cultivated, stable existence, drawing sustenance, generation after generation, from a family business, and living out its generations in the same spacious but unostentatious house. Some of its civilized urbanity and irony is suggested by the one remark that we hear of Nick's father, made to his son: " 'Whenever you feel like criticizing anyone . . . just remember that all the people in this world haven't had the advantages that you've had.' "

Fitzgerald carefully makes Nick of the third generation, which, in the folklore of such matters, is what it takes to make a "gentleman," although it is made clear that his father, a Yale graduate like the son, was also a "gentleman." In Nick's brief summary:

> My family have been prominent, well-to-do people in this Middle Western city for three generations. The Carraways are something of a clan, and we have a tradition that we're descended from the Dukes of Buccleuch, but the actual founder of my line was my grandfather's brother, who came here in fifty-one, sent a substitute to the Civil War, and started the wholesale hardware business that my father carries on today.

Midwestern Brahmanism then is the hard solid moral core of America, and it produces a Nick Carraway, whose virtues are tolerance ("all the people in the world haven't had the advantages that you've had") and honesty. These are precisely the two virtues that Fitzgerald needs in his hero: the tolerance to tolerate, and thus become involved with, the Buchanans, Jordan Baker and Gatsby, all of whom he mistrusts in varying degrees—but the honesty never to be deceived by them and, more importantly, never to be corrupted by the Buchanans and Jordan. It is one of the many ironies of the novel that Fitzgerald involves his honest hero in a brief love affair with a pathological liar.

Opposed to this specific virtuous Middle West is a rather indefinite degenerate East, although it is particularized in the one small section in which most of the novel takes place: West Egg and East Egg, New York City, and the axis—the valley of ashes, Wilson's garage, and the great staring signboard eyes of Dr. T. J. Eckleburg—that connects them.

Both Eggs represent corruption, but it is a corruption of

different orders, connected with inherited wealth on the one hand and with occupation on the other. East Egg is the home of inherited wealth, whose deeply tainted character Fitzgerald manages to suggest in a brief enumeration of names ("the Chester Beckers and the Leeches"), idiosyncrasies ("a whole clan named Blakbuck who always gathered in a corner and flipped up their noses like goats at whatsoever came near"), grotesque events ("Edgar Beaver, whose hair, they say, turned cotton-white one winter afternoon for no good reason at all") and incidental brutality ("Clarence Endive . . . had a fight with a bum named Etty in the garden"). It is in this community that Tom Buchanan, as if by instinct, settled, and when asked by Nick if he intends to stay in the East, he replies, in his best bit of self-analysis in the book, " 'I'd be a God damned fool to live anywhere else.' "

West Egg is populated by *nouveau riche*, all of whom have acquired their gains in shady or marginal activities: politicians, moving picture people, fight promoters, gamblers, bootleggers. Again Fitzgerald speaks volumes merely with nomenclature: "the Catlips and Bemburgs . . . James B. ('Rot-gut') Ferret." Farther reaches of Long Island, beyond the Eggs, are briefly suggested in the same manner ("Maurice A. Fink, and the Hammerheads, and Beluga the tobacco importer, and Beluga's girls"). It hardly needs to be pointed out that the East-West antithesis in the Eggs is a parody of the major East-West theme. According to the legend, the Easterner inherits his money, while the Westerner works for his, but the West Eggers earn their money by gambling or bootlegging.

If the essence of Midwestern Brahmanism is tolerance and honesty, as evidenced in the character of Nick Carraway, the essence of the East is summed up in the respective characters of those two expatriates from the West and South, Tom and Daisy, who between them—in his intolerance and her dishonesty—split and reverse Nick's character. In Daisy further is embodied the beauty of the East, in Tom the power, and in their union a vast irresponsibility that smashes the dream of Gatsby and finally murders the dreamer himself.

Tom Buchanan then is power and intolerance, Daisy beauty and dishonesty. His financial power is mountainous, and his physique corresponds: "you could see a great pack of muscle shifting when his shoulder moved under his coat. It was a body capable of enormous leverage—a cruel body." But this power, financial and physical, does not extend to his mind, whose powerful limitations are compensated for by a thick-skulled inflexibility. For while a libertine in action, he is in opinion a prig, faintly nourished by the thinnest pap that twentieth-century knowledge has produced, popular "scientific explanations":

> 'I read somewhere that the sun's getting hotter every year,' said Tom genially. 'It seems that pretty soon the earth's going to fall into the sun—or wait a minute—it's just the opposite—the sun's getting colder every year.'

This powerful stupidity has as its soul mate the beauty and dishonesty of Daisy. Both these characteristics of the feminine side of the equation are repeated, reemphasized, and exaggerated in Jordan Baker, who is Attractiveness gone "jaunty," "hard" and "wan," and who is Dishonesty gone pathological.

Both Jordan and Daisy are from the South, a fact which brings into view the third major American legend with which the novel deals, although the North-South relationship is the least important and the least explicit of the three. Nevertheless, it is there, despite Fitzgerald's attempt to take it away in one sentence near the end of the book. For it is part of Daisy's and Jordan's characters that they are both Southern; in Daisy's words: "From Louisville. Our white girlhood was passed together there. Our beautiful white—[here Tom interrupts her]."

In the popular mythology one of the cultural legacies bequeathed by the South to the North was the Southern belle—the beautiful, capricious, even perverse enchantress, besieged by male admirers. (Fitzgerald knew the type was not just imaginary, for he had married one.) Daisy is the lineal descendent of a society where women were lovely flowers, won after hardy pursuit by the richest or strongest male, with a solid financial contract in the background. In such a society as this, women are surrounded by an aura of mysterious beauty and inexplicable wonder, which is precisely the aura that clings to Daisy.

It was this that captivated Gatsby. Her voice echoes throughout the novel, suggesting always some surpassing, never quite clearly apprehended, enchantment. For Jordan Baker it is full of "amour"; Nick thinks it "indiscreet," although "there was an excitement in her voice that men who had cared for her found difficult to forget: a singing compulsion, a whispered 'Listen,' a promise that she had done gay, exciting things just a while since and that there were gay, exciting things hovering in the next hour." Gatsby, who perhaps in his own obsessional way knew her best, says flatly " 'Her voice is full of money,' " and this for Nick becomes the explanation.

> That was it. I'd never understood before. It was full of money—that was the inexhaustible charm that rose and fell in it, the jingle of it, the cymbal's song of it . . . High in a white palace, the king's daughter, the golden girl.

But money for Gatsby is a kind of metaphysical mystery as well, and certainly it is a synonym for beauty. It was the mysterious beauty of Daisy and her life that cast the original spell. Even her house was endowed with it:

> There was a ripe mystery about it, a hint of bedrooms upstairs more beautiful and cool than other bedrooms, of gay and radiant activities taking place through its corridors, and of romances that were not musty and laid away in lavender.

It would be a mistake of course to overemphasize the elements of the Southern legend in *The Great Gatsby*. None of the vast essential apparatus: the Civil War memories, the problems of the Negro, the decayed aristocracy, are even faintly suggested. Only the vestigial remains of the ideal of Courtly Love appear in the novel. In terms of the allegory of the novel the North-South antithesis works itself out as follows: the poor boy from the Middle West aspires to this Southern flower and, for a time, captivates her. But she is finally bought by a brutal money power from the North which transports her to a large hothouse in the East, there to ripen into a dazzling corruption. The South, in a sense, then is raped, but it desires and deserves it.

But this faint pattern is more properly a component of the larger East-West legend, which finally comes down to the fact that Easterners just "don't care," while proper Westerners do—even about the most trivial things, such as dinner. Eating with the Buchanans and Jordan, Nick thinks to himself:

> They knew that presently dinner would be over and a little later the evening, too, would be over and casually put away. It was sharply different from the West, where an evening was hurried from phase to phase toward its close, in a continually disappointed anticipation or else in sheer nervous dread of the moment itself.

And although Nick can refer to his own "provincial squeamishness" and although the Middle West can at times seem like the "ragged edge of the universe," still it is a place where one can feel, as Nick thinks when he returns there after Gatsby's tragedy, that one wants "the world to be in uniform and at a sort of moral attention forever." This image of the West as morally bracing even infects poor Wilson and his frowzy wife. Failures in the East, they had talked for ten years of going West, in order, one supposes, to be reborn. When Wilson's first suspicions about his wife are aroused, the need becomes urgent. As Wilson says to Tom: " 'I've been here too long. I want to get away. My wife and I want to go West.' "

But finally all of the internal legends are either related to or are extensions of the great legend, Gatsby's, which is the legend of America as a whole and its historical relationship to Europe.

Behind all the internal legends of *The Great Gatsby* —the legend of New York, the legends of the East vs. West and the North vs. the South—lies the greatest and most potent of American legends—the New World vs. the Old. And Gatsby himself is the key figure in Fitzgerald's interpretation of this most fundamental of American myths. Gatsby does not of course represent America, pure and simple, for, obviously, all the other characters are American as well. Yet he represents one of its most distinctive elements and, since he is the vaguest character in the book, he is also the most plainly representative one. There is also a recurring perspective in the novel as a whole through which circumstances and events and meanings become generalized and at which level America is not a conglomeration of antitheses but is an integration, any one of whose parts is representative and typical. For example, when Nick hears that Wolfsheim is the man who fixed the World Series, he reflects, somewhat piously for him: " 'It had never occurred to me that one man could start to play with the faith of fifty million people—with the single-mindedness of a burglar blowing a safe.' " The phrase "fifty million people" in the 1920's would, I suppose, refer to the entire adult population of the country, all firmly knit together in their love of baseball, in which they have entrusted their "faith." On a higher level, America is generalized and an "American character" is adduced in the splendid irony of Nick's generalization about the history of Gatsby's mansion. He is standing outside of it on a rainy afternoon and wondering how, in human reason, it had ever come into existence. He then recapitulates its history:

> There was nothing to look at from under the tree except Gatsby's enormous house, so I stared at it, like Kant at his church steeple, for half an hour. A brewer had built it early in the 'period' craze a decade before, and there was a story that he'd agree to pay five year's taxes on all the neighboring cottages if the owners would have their roofs thatched with straw. Perhaps their refusal took the heart out of his plan to Found a Family—he went into an immediate decline. His children sold his house with the black wreath still on the door.

And Nick points to the moral:

> Americans, while willing, even eager, to be serfs, have always been obstinate about being peasantry.

Again Gatsby himself is generalized as an archetype for the young American male. Watching Gatsby in his car Nick thinks:

> He was balancing himself on the dashboard of his car with the resourcefulness of movement that is so peculiarly American—that comes, I suppose, with the absence of lifting work in youth and, even more, with the formless grace of our nervous, sporadic games. This quality was continually breaking through his punctilious manner in the shape of restlessness.

And finally Gatsby himself *thinks* (if he may be properly said to think) of himself as an American archetype: "He sprang from his own Platonic conception of himself." He is an individual in search of a myth. And he tries many—Ben Franklin's prudence and hard work, adventuring with Dan Cody, the life of a soldier-hero in the war, an Oxford graduate, a young American prince in Europe, and finally that of a free-spending American millionaire. Yet in all his mythological masks—"diving bells"—as Thomas Mann calls them, Gatsby is searching for some supreme, unutterable consummation, whose final object lies far beyond and above the lovely, mortal clay of Daisy who is its ostensible object.

Gatsby, as has often been said, represents the irony of American history and the corruption of the American dream. While this certainly is true, yet even here, with this general legend, Fitzgerald has rung in his own characteristic changes, doubling and redoubling ironies. At the center of the legend proper there is the relationship between Europe and America and the ambiguous interaction between the contradictory impulses of Europe that led to the original settling of America and its subsequent development: mercantilism and idealism. At either end of American history, and all the way through, the two impulses have a way of being both radically exclusive and mutually confusing, the one melting into the other: the human faculty of wonder, on the one hand, and the power and beauty of things, on the other.

The Great Gatsby dramatizes this continuing ambiguity directly in the life of Gatsby and retrospectively by a glance at history at the end of the novel. Especially does it do so in the two passages in the novel of what might be called the ecstatic moment, the moment when the human imagination seems to be on the verge of entering the earthly paradise. The two passages are (1) the real Gatsby looking on the real Daisy, and (2) the imaginary Dutchmen, whom Nick conjures up at the end of the novel, looking on the "green breast" of Long Island.

Here is the description of Gatsby and Daisy.

> Out of the corner of his eye Gatsby saw that the blocks of the sidewalk really formed a ladder and mounted to a secret place above the trees—he could climb to it, if he climbed alone, and once there he could suck on the pap of life, gulp down the incomparable milk of wonder.
>
> His heart beat faster and faster as Daisy's white face came up to his own. He knew that when he kissed this girl, and forever wed his unutterable visions to her perishable breath, his mind would never romp again like the mind of God. So he waited, listening for a moment longer to the tuning-fork that had been struck upon a star. Then he kissed her. At his lips' touch she blossomed for him like a flower and the incarnation was complete.

And here is Nick's imaginative reconstruction of the legendary Dutchman. He is sprawled on the sand at night, with Gatsby's mansion behind him and Long Island Sound in front of him.

> And as the moon rose higher the inessential houses began to melt away until gradually I became aware of the old Island that flowered once for Dutch eyes—a fresh green breast of the new world. Its vanished trees, the trees that had made way for Gatsby's house, had once pandered in whispers to the last and greatest of all human dreams; for a transitory enchanted moment man must have held his breath in the presence of this continent, compelled into an aesthetic contemplation he neither understood nor desired, face to face for the last time in history with something commensurate to his capacity for wonder.

The repetition in the two passages of the words "wonder" and "flower" hardly need comment, or the sexuality, illicit in the Dutchmen's and both infantile and mature in Gatsby's—or the star-lit, moon-lit setting in both. For these are the central symbols in the book: the boundless imagination trying to transfigure under the stars the endlessly beautiful object. Now, of course, the Dutchmen and Gatsby are utterly different types of being and going in different directions. The Dutchmen are pure matter, momentarily and unwillingly raised into the realms of the spirit, while Gatsby is pure spirit coming down to earth. They pass one another, so to speak, at the moment when ideal and reality seem about to converge. Historically, the Dutch, legendarily stolid, pursued their mercantile ways and produced finally a Tom Buchanan but also, it should be remembered, a Nick Carraway. But their ecstatic moment hung on in the air, like an aroma, intoxicating prophets, sages, poets, even poor farm boys in twentieth-century Dakota. The heady insubstantiability of the dream and the heavy intractability of the reality were expressed by Van Wyck Brooks (who could well have been Fitzgerald's philosopher in these matters) in his *The Wine of the Puritans* as follows:

> You put the old wine [Europeans] into new bottles [American continent] . . . and when the explosion results, one may say, the aroma passes into the air and the wine spills on the floor. The aroma or the ideal, turns into transcendentalism and the wine or the real, becomes commercialism.

No one knew better than Gatsby that nothing could finally match the splendors of his own imagination, and the novel would suggest finally that not only had the American dream been corrupted but that it was, in part anyway, necessarily corrupted, for it asked too much. Nothing of this earth, even the most beautiful of earthly objects, could be anything but a perversion of it.

The Great Gatsby, then, begins in a dramatization, as suggested, of the basic thesis of the early Van Wyck

Brooks: that America had produced an idealism so impalpable that it had lost touch with reality (Gatsby) and a materialism so heavy that it was inhuman (Tom Buchanan). The novel as a whole is another turn of the screw on this legend, with the impossible idealism trying to realize itself, to its utter destruction, in the gross materiality. As Nick says of Gatsby at the end of the novel,

> his dream must have seemed so close that he could hardly fail to grasp it. He did not know that it was already behind him back in that vast obscurity beyond the city, where the dark fields of the republic rolled on under the night.

Yet he imagines too that Gatsby, before his moment of death, must have had his "realization" of the intractable brutishness of matter,

> he must have felt that he had lost the old warm world, paid a high price for living too long with a single dream. He must have looked up at an unfamiliar sky through frightening leaves and shivered as he found what a grotesque thing a rose is and how raw the sunlight was upon the scarcely created grass.

Thus Fitzgerald multiplies the ironies of the whole legend: that the mercantile Dutchmen should have been seduced into the esthetic; that Gatsby's wondrous aspirations should attach themselves to a Southern belle and that in pursuit of her he should become a gangster's lieutenant; that young Englishmen ("agonizingly aware of the easy money in the vicinity") should scramble for crumbs at Gatsby's grandiose parties (the Dutchmen once more); that idealism, beauty, power, money should get all mixed up; that history should be a kind of parody of itself, as with the case of the early Dutch and the contemporary English explorers.

Still *The Great Gatsby* would finally suggest, at a level beyond all its legends and in the realm of the properly tragic, that it is right and fitting that the Jay Gatzes of the world should ask for the impossible, even when they do so as pathetically and ludicrously as does Gatsby himself.

Writing to Fitzgerald about his novel, Maxwell Perkins, after enumerating some specific virtues, said,

> these are such things as make a man famous. And all the things, the whole pathetic episode, you have given a place in time and space, for with the help of T. J. Eckleburg, and by an occasional glance at the sky, or the city, you have imparted a sort of sense of eternity.

A "sense of eternity"—this is indeed high praise, but I think that Perkins, as he often was, was right.

For at its highest level *The Great Gatsby* does not deal with local customs or even national and international legends but with the permanent realities of existence. On this level nothing or nobody is to blame, and people are what they are and life is what it is, just as, in Bishop Butler's words, "things are what they are." At this level, too, most people don't count; they are merely a higher form of animality living out its mundane existence: the Tom Buchanans, the Jordan Bakers, the Daisy Fays. Only Nick and Gatsby count. For Gatsby, with all his absurdities and his short, sad, pathetic life, is still valuable; in Nick's parting words to him: "You're worth the whole damn bunch put together." Nick, who in his way is as much of this world as Daisy is in hers, still sees, obscurely, the significance of Gatsby. And although he knows that the content of Gatsby's dream is corrupt, he senses that its form is pristine. For, in his own fumbling, often gross way, Gatsby was obsessed with the wonder of human life and driven by the search to make that wonder actual. It is the same urge that motivates visionaries and prophets, the urge to make the facts of life measure up to the splendors of the human imagination, but it is utterly pathetic in Gatsby's case because he is trying to do it so subjectively and so uncouthly, and with dollar bills. Still Nick's obscure instinct that Gatsby is essentially all right is sound. It often seems as if the novel is about the contrast between the two, but the bond between them reveals that they are not opposites but rather complements, opposed together, to all the other characters in the novel.

Taken together they contain most of the essential polarities that go to make up the human mind and its existence. Allegorically considered, Nick is reason, experience, waking, reality, and history, while Gatsby is imagination, innocence, sleeping, dream, and eternity. Nick is like Wordsworth listening to "the still sad music of humanity," while Gatsby is like Blake seeing hosts of angels in the sun. The one can only look at the facts and see them as tragic; the other tries to transform the facts by an act of the imagination. Nick's mind is conservative and historical, as is his lineage; Gatsby's is radical and apocalyptic—as rootless as his heritage. Nick is too much immersed in time and in reality; Gatsby is hopelessly out of it. Nick is always withdrawing, while Gatsby pursues the green light. Nick can't be hurt, but neither can he be happy. Gatsby can experience ecstasy, but his fate is necessarily tragic. They are generically two of the best types of humanity: the moralist and the radical.

One may well ask why, if their mental horizons are so lofty, is one a bond salesman and the other a gangster's lieutenant, whose whole existence is devoted to a love affair that has about it the unmistakable stamp of adolescence? The answer is, I think, that Fitzgerald did not know enough of what a philosopher or revolutionary might really be like, that at this point in his life he must have always thought of love in terms of a Princeton Prom, and that, writing in the twenties, a bond salesman and a gangster's functionary would seem more representative anyway. Van Wyck Brooks might have said, at one time, that his culture gave him nothing more to work with. A lesser writer might have attempted to make Nick a literal sage and Gatsby a literal prophet. But it is certain that such a thought would never have entered Fitzgerald's head, as he was only dramatizing the morals and manners of the life he knew. The genius of the novel consists precisely in the fact that, while using only the stuff, one might better say the froth and flotsam of its own limited time and place, it has managed to suggest, as Perkins said, a sense of eternity.

**THE DAMNATION
OF THERON WARE**

THE DAMNATION OF THERON WARE is such
an interesting novel and so neglected a minor classic that
one hardly knows how to begin talking about it. Those
who have read it sympathetically can only nod in wise
agreement about the intricacies of its narration and its wry
ironies, its humor and its ultimate terror. There is a Theron Ware in all of us, a capacity for pride and its consequence, damnation. And this pride is of the most inviting
and powerful kind—not pride of place or position or
wealth, but pride of the intellect: the beguilingly insidious
idea that we know more than others and are somehow
wiser and better than they are. Other people should auto-
matically admire us, and our inner life should likewise be
a kind of pleasing dream, without the prehistoric monsters
or the modern gargoyles always looming up in the shadows behind and around us.

Pride and its deceptiveness are, of course, the subject of
all serious literature, from *Oedipus Rex* through *Faust* to
Remembrance of Things Past. One might go further and
say that some form of deception is the basis for all literature. At a high level it consists of tragic irony, the deception of the hero, as in *Oedipus*; at a low level it consists of
plain mystification, the deception of the reader, as in the
detective story. But what lends *The Damnation* its unique
character, and I know of nothing else in literature quite
like it, is the fact that it falls exactly halfway between
these two extremes. It is the story of a Faust, albeit a

rather sorry one, who aspires to a cultural perspective and to a woman who embodies it that are far too rich for his rather meager blood. In its pursuit he becomes puffed up, physically as well as mentally, alienates himself from his simple, sturdy wife, becomes contemptuous of the Methodist religion, of which he is an ordained minister, and of the Philistinism of his own flock, lusts after the person of Celia Madden, a rich red-headed Irish Catholic beauty, and after the learning of Father Forbes, an urbane and skeptical priest—then his terrible fall: to be told by Celia that she does not love him, that far from developing he has been degenerating, and that he has become—that most unbearable of truths—a "bore."

Yet we do not stand outside this process and look down at the hero, always knowing more than he does; we are involved to a degree in Theron's own lack of perception. This is the detective-story aspect, although *The Damnation* is no mystery story either. All the proper evidence is there, but there are two sets of evidence, one for the appearance of things, and the other for the reality of things. Theron has only the appearance, and we see both; yet while we know what the reality is, the appearance begiles us as well or, to put it another way, it keeps raising questions in our minds. For example, the novel was published in England under the title *The Illumination*, and when we put the English title and the American title together we have the paradox of "Illumination-Damnation." For what happens to Theron is also an illumination that casts relentless and searching light on the illiberal fanaticism of his religion and on the paltriness and inflexibility of his upper-New York State rural background. When Theron reads Renan's autobiography, that of an apostate who deeply loved the church from which he defected, when he hears Father Forbes or Dr. Ledsmar, Forbes's learned and scientific friend, discourse on history or religion or science, when Celia clad in Grecian robes plays Chopin for him, the scales drop from his eyes. He even expands physically, becoming more impressive and able to deliver eloquent sermons to his own flock (this is the appearance), but Celia's dying brother Michael tells him that whereas he used to have a saintly countenance, he now has the face of a "bar-keeper" (this is the reality). Still it is true that he is a more effective preacher and that his mental horizon has become immensely wider. Again there is a chain of evidence presented to Theron, and the reader, to make him suspect that there is a covert relationship between Alice, his wife, and Levi Gorringe, the town lawyer. And again this evidence has a most persuasive appearance, although the reality—our knowledge of the simple goodness and steadfastness of Alice's character—should tell us differently, and it does so, but not without leaving some ambiguous question marks dangling in the now sulphurous atmosphere. There is a third false hare started by evidences that the beautiful Celia *does*, in fact, love Theron. Indeed the scene in which she plays him Chopin is positively prurient. What, we may ask, is the poor man, a farm boy and a Methodist minister, to think? He should have remembered—but, like all of us, he has a tendency to forget the little but significant unpleasant-ries—that after a passionate declaration on his part of his becoming a lover of the Greeks, as is she, she yawns. This points squarely to that terrible denouement, whose cli-matic word is "bore."

These ambiguities are further enhanced by the charac-ter of the protagonist himself, who is simultaneously lik-able and despicable. The ambiguous hero was one of Frederic's fortes, and the only other novel of interest that he wrote, *Seth's Brother's Wife*, interesting chiefly be-cause it is a flawed precursor of *The Damnation*, likewise has a hero whom we both like and despise. *Seth's Broth-er's Wife*, a first novel, ended happily with the hero saved and forgiven. But by the time of writing *The Damnation* (1896), Frederic had grown wiser and gave his protagonist the ending he deserved. Still, we cannot help feeling some ineradicable sympathy for Theron and in a peculiar, unex-plainable way like him. We are glad to see him alive at the end of the novel—he had tried unsuccessfully to com-mit suicide after Celia told him the truth—reunited with

Alice, and on his way to Seattle to go into real estate although we know that he will in all likelihood make an ass out of himself all over again and probably mistreat Alice again, as she prophesies in the last sentence of the book. In fact already he has begun to see himself as a political figure in the Northwest, using for political purposes the oratorical powers that once captivated Methodists. He sees in a vision a vast multitude transfixed by the eloquence of his rhetoric and the play of his shapely, white, well-manicured hand.

Our lingering sympathy for him, despite the fact that he is a mountebank, a bore, and at the height of his illumination-damnation "the meanest man in town," results from two factors. First of all, he is incurably boyish. He brings out the mother-impulse of all the women in the book, who think of him as a nice young man of certain potentialities if only a wise woman can take him in hand. Thus his "damnation" is not final, but provisional, and he is still at the end a "boy," albeit a bit tarnished now. A second and deeper reason for our lingering sympathy arises out of the very method of narration, described above. According to Aristotle's formula, we feel pity and terror at the hero's fall—pity because a man has fallen, terror because he is a man like ourselves, and his misfortune could be ours. The pity is our objective, social reaction, in which our deepest self is not involved, while the terror is our subjective, personal reaction bound up with our deepest fears. In other words, through pity, we stand back from the tragic hero while, through terror, we identify ourselves with him. But in *The Damnation* the distancing factor, the superiority of our knowledge over that of Oedipus, is missing, for we are partially involved in his misperceptions. Further we are involved with a character whose misapprehension is not about a set of facts but about the nature of reality, which is our own deepest, most difficult, and most terrifying problem. Pity then is out of the question; we can feel only the terror. And indeed in the middle of the book the reader, if he be honest, begins to wonder about himself. I know of no other novel in which this device of involving the reader in the imperceptions of the protagonist is so artfully and so fairly done, and yet no other novel that is so puzzling, without being at all incomprehensible, in its earlier parts. So skilfully is it all done that even when we are sure that Theron is completely wrong and is "damned," even after trustworthy and perceptive characters in the novel tell him so, we still feel a lingering ambiguity and we still feel, against all evidence and all odds, that perhaps he *has* been illuminated and that Celia *does* love him. Only at the very end are all suspicions allayed. This is so, I think, because we are always saying to ourselves, consciously or unconsciously, *de te fabula.*

If *The Damnation* is unique in structure and psychology, it is unique as a cultural document as well. It exists on three historical and cultural levels: first, it emanates very clearly from late nineteenth-century America; second, it is also concerned with that perennial theme of much serious American literature: what is the identity and the nature of "the American" and what is his relationship to Europe? and, third, it is a metaphorical statement about the essential polarities of all human existence.

On the first historical level *The Damnation* is about how the powerful, relentless, experienced intellect of the late nineteenth century, combined with its love of "art for art," seduced, quickened, and finally damned the lingering intuitionalism and the reliance upon feelings, and the anti-aestheticism, which were the legacy of the early nineteenth and of which Theron Ware is the anachronistic embodiment. For Theron is the poor vessel for two outbursts of emotionalism that occurred in the late eighteenth and early nineteenth centuries: Methodism in the Protestant religion and the Romantic love of Nature.

Frederic is careful to make Theron and his Methodism as concrete and as historically accurate as possible. By the late nineteenth century, when *The Damnation* takes place, the genuineness of the old Methodist fervor had gone, while the essential emphasis on individual feeling and the general intolerance had remained. When we first meet the Methodists in *The Damnation,* we are told that their faces were "remarkable for goodness, candor, self-complacency, rather than learning or mental astuteness." This sight was a pleasant prospect in the oldest men, some of whom had been ordained by men who had known Francis Asbury "and even Whitefield," for they represented the rude energy, poverty, devotion of the Westward-moving pioneers. But the middle-aged Methodists were merely fat and prosperous, and with each generation moral fervor seemed to decrease, while the narrow fanaticism, often allied now to commercial instincts and purposes, still remained.

Moreover, Theron's congregation in Octavius was a special case of arrested development. The novel takes place in the 1870's or 1880's. Sometime in the 1850's, during the violent ruptures and the battle of the "isms" that preceded the Civil War, there had been a schism within the Methodist Episcopal Church itself. The advancing sophistication and liberalism of the majority, now on its way to becoming the Methodist Church of today, disconcerted a minority of literal believers who wished to restore the Church to primitive Methodism. This argument was settled by the defection of the great Southern branch over the issue of States' Rights and by the defection of the Northern malcontents into a new Church, Free Methodism. But Octavius was one of those places where the dissident minority, the "primitives," had remained within the Church and, like all determined minorities, succeeded in controlling it. Theron, who has the outlook but none of the strength of the old Methodists, is thus at their mercy and at the mercy of the waywardness of his own instincts.

He is anachronistic, too, in that he is an Emersonian, a Romantic, a lover of nature, which he thinks somehow will sustain and fortify him. What matter anyone's ideas of Hell, he says, looking up at the trees and the leaves and the sky, when we have all this to look at—and then, the damning words: " 'It seems to me that we never *feel* [italics Frederic's] quite so sure of God's goodness at other times as we do in these wonderful new mornings of spring.' " Frederic plays up the anachronism by describing Theron's reaction to nature in the early stages of the book in the rhetoric of eighteenth-century nature poetry: "the birds sang in tireless choral confusion"; and "The gay clamor of the woodland songsters." As his damnation proceeds apace, his love of nature becomes more extravagant and after a perfunctory kiss from Celia, which sealed his doom, becomes positively pantheistic. At night alone he bows his head to the moon and addresses it as "God." But after his fall he is no longer a Methodist, believing in the sanctity of feelings, or an Emersonian, believing in the beneficence of nature. The look in his eyes had changed: "They did not dwell fondly upon the picture of the lofty, spreading boughs, with their waves of sap-green leafage against the blue. They did not soften and glow this time, at the thought of how wholly one felt sure of God's goodness in these wonderful new mornings of spring." In other words, Theron, not a strong creature at best, is a historical anachronism as well, representing the vestigial remains of the consciousness of the early nineteenth century, once powerful, now vulnerable.

He is subjected to three forces peculiar to the late nineteenth century, each of which represents a negation of his own beliefs and tenets. I refer here to the influences of Celia and Dr. Ledsmar, deferring a discussion of the role of Father Forbes until later. Two of these forces are embodied in Celia, reinforced, it must be insisted upon, by her physical beauty. Historically, she represents a phenomenon that occurred in the late nineteenth century when, as a reaction against utilitarianism, rationalism, and relativism, Catholicism *cum* Art emerged with a vengeance. Despite the fact that Celia is Irish and American, she bears the stamp of late nineteenth-century English culture and brings up memories of the Pre-Raphaelites and the *Yellow Book* and Aubrey Beardsley, redolent of secular incense, private altars, diabolical poetry devoted to God, pictures of the Virgin overhanging nude statuary (a phenomenon which is the principal feature of Celia's inner temple), drunkards in penitential sackcloth, erotic celibates writing obscure verse about the Trinity, the obscene and the sacred marching hand in hand, indeed, joined together in fast union against the intolerably dull and sanctimonious bourgeoisie. Celia herself, it must be admitted, is the Achilles heel of the novel, never quite credible and always verging on the preposterous. Frederic's style, never distinguished except in dialogue, falters badly when dealing with her. But her effect on Theron is overwhelming. And when he sees her inner temple, with its pictures of the Virgin and its nude statuary, and hears Chopin, he almost faints and declares soulfully to his "Hellenizer," " 'I want to be a Greek myself, if you're one. I want to get as close to you—to your ideal, that is, as I can.' " (It is here that she yawns.) His puritanical Methodism has been overwhelmed by the sights and sounds of Beauty and by the magnificence of Beauty's High Priestess, Celia, and lurking about it all, leering at him from out of the shadows, is the sense of the forbidden.

Dr. Ledsmar, on the other hand, represents the professionalism and scientism of nineteenth-century Germany, which looks upon nature not as a pantheistic embodiment of God, but as a vast puzzle whose secrets are to be extracted only by rigorous, dispassionate, ruthless trial and experiment. Thus when Theron, the nature-lover, goes to visit the Doctor, he sees a lot of flowers and remarks that the Doctor must be a lover of flowers. To the contrary, Ledsmar replies, " 'My work is to test the probabilities for or against Darwin's theory that hermaphroditism in plants is a late by-product of these earlier forms.' " When Theron politely asks if the theory is correct, Ledsmar replies that they will know in three or four hundred years. Still later they come upon the supine and senseless body of Ledsmar's Chinese servant, looking as if dead. The Doctor examines his servant, takes his pulse, and jots down the findings in a notebook, explaining to Theron that he is loading the man with doses of opium that would be lethal to an Occidental, all in the interests of science. In other realms Dr. Ledsmar is equally disconcerting. When Theron conceives the idea of writing a book about Abraham,

Dr. Ledsmar, who is also a leading Assyriologist, reels off a list of authorities in German, a language Theron cannot read. Indeed, every time that Theron meets the Doctor, Ledsmar delivers himself of a series of learned, persuasive, startling statements, about religion or women or history, that come as a series of intellectual shocks to Theron and make him feel like the schoolboy that he is. Thus in the meetings between the two men we see professional learning and science breaking down the defenses of the last traces of Romantic intuitionalism; it is the post-Darwinian expressing his disdain for the pre-Darwinian. So uncommitted to anything but science is Dr. Ledsmar that there is a touch of the diabolical about him. His one book, he tells Theron, was on serpent-worship, and it is he who christens Theron himself *diabolus* in the most gruesome symbol in the novel. The Doctor has no doubt that Theron is on his way to damnation, and after Theron leaves his house after their last meeting he goes to a tank and takes out a lizard, "long, slim, yellowish-green . . . with a coiling, sensuous tail and a pointed evil head." " 'Yes, you are the type,' " he says to the reptile. " 'Your name isn't Johnny any more. It's the Rev. Theron Ware.' "

On its second historical level *The Damnation* is concerned with the relationship of America to Europe; here again it is unique and for two reasons. First, it shows Irish Catholicism conquering American Protestantism, a happening without parallel in an important American novel, and, second, it has put together in the same book the respective viewpoints of Henry James and Mark Twain.

Theron had grown up with the standard nineteenth-century Protestant-American concept of the Irish-Catholics. Thus when he inadvertently witnesses the last rites of the Catholic Church being performed by the urbane and commanding Father Forbes, he is pleasantly surprised by the dignity, solemnity, and Latinity of the ceremony. On this same occasion he has met the beautiful and sophisticated Celia. Are these, then, the drunken, boorish Irish of his imagination—sinister and repellent, denizens of the city warrens where they wallow in crime and corrupt politics? (Now that he thinks of it he has never known anybody who was not a Republican.) Still the lurid image suspends itself in his imagination, "sculptured rows of lowering, ape-like faces . . . and out of these sprang into the vague upper gloom, on the one side, lamp-posts from which negroes hung by the neck, and on the other gibbets for dynamiters and Molly Maguires; and between the two glowed a spectral picture of some black-robed, tonsured men, with leering satanic masks, making a bonfire of the Bible in public schools." Then he goes to visit Father Forbes at evening. There is an electric door-bell, a modern, sophisticated device which Theron has never seen before. Inside, Father Forbes and his learned, skeptical friend, Dr. Ledsmar, are having their dinner together—this at night rather than at noon as with Protestants. They are drinking wine and eating subtly prepared food. The conversation is startling. Theron is literally terrorized and almost runs from the room when Father Forbes tells him that if historians could get back far enough, " 'we should find whole receding series of types of this Christ-myth of ours.' " Dr. Ledsmar delivers himself of a series of his characteristically unorthodox opinions. He explains to Theron, among other things, that Father Forbes never preaches to his parishioners because most of them would not understand him and those that did would complain about his heterodoxy. Theron finds out later that both Celia and Father Forbes are given to rather startling and unsettling prophecies about Catholicism. Celia informs him that she, and those like her, will transform the religion itself by eradicating the gloomy, ascetic, art-hating propensities of the early Church Fathers and by introducing art, beauty, and sex. Father Forbes predicts that someday the world will sicken of the sect-squabbling and Biblical-wrangling of the Protestants and will then return to Mother Church, where you have nothing to do but " 'be aggreable, and avoid scandal, and observe the covenances.' " Father Forbes further prophesies that the Irish Catholics will finally conquer America, and he explains the basis for this prediction in quite naturalistic terms. In America the Kelt had discovered the Teuton drink, beer, which was suited to his mercurial nature, as the disastrous whiskey was not. From this conjunction of the Irish race and the Teuton drink would issue forth a new race, a new church, a new nation: Irish-Catholic-America: " 'The lager-drinking Irishman in a few generations will be a new type of humanity—the Kelt at his best. He will dominate America. He will be *the* American. And his church—with the Italian element thrown clean out of it, and its Pope living, say, in Baltimore or Georgetown—will be the church of America.' "

In most American novels these passages would be nonsense and the intent of the author satiric. But this is not the case in *The Damnation*, where everything that Father Forbes says is to be attended to. When this same outlook is personified by the sexually alluring Celia, the results for the young American Methodist are literally maddening. Looked at from this point of view, the novel would appear to be an idiosyncratic *lapsus naturae*, novelistically speaking, in which for practically the only time in American literature an Irish-Catholic rather than American-Protestant view of things was adopted, and complex Irish Catholicism was shown corrupting simple American Methodism, as indeed in part is the case.

Looked at from another perspective, however, *The Damnation* proves not to be a freak, but rather central for American culture, and here the comparison and contrast with Henry James is apt.

Whether Frederic himself really believed in the prophecies and partook of the point of view of Father Forbes and Celia, we shall never know, although we do know that, while neither Irish nor Catholic, Frederic himself was an admirer of the "Kelt." But the question itself is beside the point, for *The Damnation* is concerned not so much with the religious as with the cultural. It is one of the many anomalies of the novel that while most of its principal characters are connected with a religion, no one, except Alice Ware, seems to believe in God, at least in any literal sense. Theron himself comes to realize this when he is wandering around in the lower depths of New York after his "fall," trying unsuccessfully to get drunk. Here in these Dostoevskian regions, he sees for the first time what a real belief in God means. This is his only genuine perception in the book as a whole.

> "I've been drinking for two days and one whole night, on my feet all the while, wandering alone in that big strange New York, going through places where they murdered men for ten cents, mixing myself up with the worst people in low bar-houses and dance-houses, and they saw I had money in my pocket, too,—and yet nobody touched me, or offered to lay a finger on me. Do you know why? They understood that I wanted to get drunk, and couldn't. The Indians won't harm an idiot, or lunatic, you know. Well, it was the same with these vilest of the vile. They saw that I was a fool whom God had taken hold of, to break his heart first, and then to craze his brain, and then to fling him on a dunghill to die, like a dog. They believe in God, these people. They're the only ones who do, it seems to me."

And the real problems in the novel are not religious but are rather Jamesian and cultural, not whether God exists but how should man live.

The Damnation, in part at least, is really the story of *Roderick Hudson*, only told in an indigenous setting. The resemblances between it and James's first full-scale novel are remarkable: Theron is Roderick, the gifted but unstable young man who collapses in the face of a deeper, wider, richer culture than the one into which he had been born; Celia Madden is Christina Light, the sexual embodiment of this culture; Father Forbes and Dr. Ledsmar are Gloriani, the elder statesmen and spokesmen for it; Alice Ware is Mary Garland, the simple, honest, none-too-attractive-sexually American girl who is left behind; the Nedahma Methodist Church, Theron's congregation, is Northhampton, Massachusetts, Roderick's home town; the Irish Catholic Church, Theron's nemesis; the culture of Italy, Roderick's; both protagonists first undergo a quickening effect and then are doomed, Theron to an ignominious collapse in a New York hotel room and Roderick to suicide in the Italian Alps. Thus James's great theme is duplicated almost point by point in *The Damnation* without any of the characters ever setting foot aboard ship.

But, in contradistinction to James and more like Mark Twain, Frederic's answer to Europe, his "heiress of all the ages," was not a Milly Theale or a Maggie Verver; rather she is Sister Soulsby, a middle-aged Methodist fund-raiser with a dubious past and a common-law marriage. In *The Damnation* she is the polar opposite to Father Forbes—a Newman, let us say, confronting a Gloriani, although the direct confrontation never takes place in Frederic's novel, as it never does in a direct sense in the work of James.

Sister Soulsby, however, does not descend, in all her strength, from the Emersonian air of America, as do the strong Americans in James; on the contrary she arises from the harsh struggle of its often bitter earth. When Theron first meets her, she passes herself off as that most pathetic and romantic of American fictions, the dispossessed Southern belle. But when she tells him her real story, after she has taken a liking to him and after she has decided to straighten him out, she speaks the real idiom. Her story likewise is idiomatic: a run-away from a "stupid" home with a married man, leading lady in comic opera companies in the West, fortuneteller in the gold country, professional clairvoyant, professional medium, once within one vote of being indicted by a grand jury, the dissenting vote having been bought up by a train gambler who finally died with his boots on, taking three sheriff's deputies with him to eternity. Likewise her mate, Brother Soulsby, has had a non-Emersonian career: actor, phrenologist, advance agent for the British Blondes show, lecturer on female diseases, and one-time invited guest of a grand jury. They had first met when Brother Soulsby was lecturing on female diseases, had taken a liking to one another, and had agreed to "retire" together, he to a garden that he had always wanted to plant, she to books that she had always wanted to read. The ineptness of a Methodist meeting, witnessed by chance, had aroused their professional instincts and had determined them to take these amateurs in hand and show them what professional organization could do.

Sister Soulsby is the voice of shrewd, pragmatic wisdom and is possessed of a genius for getting things done. Her own private religion is simple, moral rather than theological: " 'I've got a religion of my own, and its got just one plank in it, and that is that the time to separate the sheep from the goats is on Judgment Day, and that it can't be done a minute before.' "

Her speech is right out of Mark Twain, as is her attitude. After she has patched up everything for Theron, brought the hostile Methodists around to him and raised the money to pay off a great part of the church debt—she comes on the scene when he is most in trouble as a minister—she tells him: " 'The result was you went through as if you'd had your ears pinned back, and been greased all over,' " as indeed he had. Just about all institutions, she tells Theron, are frauds, as are many of the people who make them. The analogy that she uses is the stage. To one sitting in the audience everything looks real, but backstage are the Sister Soulsbys, who really run things, and they know that the trees and houses are cloth, and the moon is tissue paper and the flying fairy is a middle-aged woman strung up on a rope. But that does not matter, for "organization" is the secret of strength, and only it gets things done. Instead of accepting this elementary fact the Theron Wares want to sit down and weep because the moon is not a real moon. She and Brother Soulsby do good and help other people, without worrying about the fraudulence of the institution they must employ.

Sister Soulsby is every bit as influential on Theron Ware as are Father Forbes, Ledsmar, and Celia, and constitutes their antidote. There is hardly a word that she utters to Theron that he does not take as gospel, and it is she who teaches him how to be a success at his job. Later, after his fall, it is Sister Soulsby to whom he instinctively turns as the only person in the world who will still think of him as a human being. When she greets the bloated, dirty, sodden wreck who was once Theron Ware, he gasps: " 'I have come out of hell, for the sake of having some human being speak to me like that!' " It is Sister Soulsby who restores his confidence and Brother Soulsby who gets him into business in Seattle.

The Damnation then is not only the story of *Roderick Hudson*, it is also the story of *Huckleberry Finn*, the triumph of pragmatic wisdom, not learned from ideals but wrested from often grimy circumstances in an unsettled, expanding, traditionless culture. Like Huck, the Soulsbys have learned to bend to the wind and to tell the necessary lies, while always preserving an inner integrity and a moral purpose of their own. Like Huck, they are inclined to think the respectable world, of businessmen with their cravats and ministers in their top hats, a bit ridiculous. The one person in the novel who is always having a good time is Brother Soulsby, whose amusement at the antics of the righteous is unbounded although he can beat them at their own game. While he hardly ever says anything—he is a small, quiet, efficient man—we always know there is a twinkle in his eye. The one time he openly laughs is when he reports to Sister Soulsby the identity of the nocturnal caller, who is poor Theron: "Brother Soulsby cackled in merriment. 'It's Brother Ware of Octavius, out on a little bat, all by himself. He says he's been on the loose only two days but it looks more like a fortnight.' " When Sister Soulsby asks him for an explanation of this extraordinary event, Brother Soulsby replies with his characteristic wisdom and humor: " 'Well, he explains it pretty badly, if you ask me. . . . But don't think I suggested any explanations. I've been a mother myself. He's merely filled himself up to the neck with rum, in the simple, ordinary, good old-fashioned way. That's all. What is there to explain about that?' " Under the ministrations of the Soulsbys, the Huck Finns, Theron, instead of committing suicide, is restored, partially at least, goes off to Seattle to start all over, wiser, if sadder. In this fact resides the genius of the Soulsbys; they don't expect anything or anybody to be perfect and merely try to salvage as much good as they can from the materials at hand. They represent a point of view that crops up in other places in American literature as well; it is usually expressed in prosaic metaphor, the imagery coming from the soil or hand labor. " 'My dear friend,' " says Sister Soulsby to Theron, " 'you might just as well say that potatoes are unclean and unfit to eat because manure is put into the ground they grow in.' " The same idea is expressed in another context by Robert Morss Lovett as the concluding sentence of his excellent introduction to the 1924 edition of *The Damnation*; "If only Woodrow Wilson had taken Sister Soulsby to Paris!" (p. xii).

Does this mean then that Sister Soulsby or what she represents is to be taken as the "moral" of the novel? The answer is "No," for hers is only one point of view, sane but grubby, in a novel that has no moral or message save the rather grim reminder that man is a poor creature, generally speaking, and is always being tempted to run off after pleasing illusions and to be blind to harsh realities. There is, nevertheless, a hierarchy of outlook and point of view, with some outlooks obviously more valuable and possessed of more strength than others. Theron's, of course, would be the lowest, while the respective attitudes of Father Forbes and Sister Soulsby would be the highest and strongest. And these two people, in turn, are the most powerful influences upon Theron. Ledsmar's influence is more disconcerting than anything else, and Celia exerts her strongest pull on a physiological rather than an ideological level. As such, Celia's is the most powerful of all, but it is brief and crushingly frustrated, and must diminish as the years go by, while what Father Forbes and Sister Soulsby tell him he must carry, ever fresh, to the grave. If we consider the novel in this way, the real lines of force could be represented diagrammatically as an inverted triangle, with Theron at the upside-down apex and Father Forbes and Sister Soulsby at the two end-points of the upraised base. Thus two very different lines of force, coming from widely separate directions, run down to Theron.

The triangle then would appear to be incomplete, lacking a straight, horizontal line between the priest and the Methodist fund-raiser. But there is an unseen line here as well which Dr. Ledsmar points to, even though there is never any actual meeting between the "Father" and the "Sister."

Primarily Father Forbes is the voice of Catholicism, although of a very heterodox and sophisticated kind. His deepest influence on Theron, however, is not religious but historical. The key is given in the first conversation between the two. Theron has just witnessed the solemn Last Rites, and he remarks to the priest on their impressiveness. Father Forbes replies: " 'It is a very ancient ceremony . . . probably Persian like the baptismal form, although, for that matter, we can never dig deep enough for the roots of these things. They all turn up Turanian if we probe far enough.' " Theron thinks nothing of this remark at the time, but it has sunk deep into his progressivist soul and disturbed it deeply, as subsequent events show. Later at home he rereads the thirteen chapters in Genesis which chronicle the story of Abraham. He notices for the first time that Abraham was not a Jew but a Chaldean, as was his brother, Lot's father. Hitherto Theron had thought there had been Jews from the beginning or at least, say, from the Flood. If this came as a surprise to him, would it not come likewise as a slight shock to the rest of the world? He would write a learned book about the Chaldeans. Then reality thrusts forward its strong, ugly face, as Theron suddenly realizes his own ignorance and lack of learning. It is at this point that the memory of his encounter with Father Forbes returns, and he realizes that all this mental activity had been stared off by "the chance remark of the Romish priest" about the Turanians, of whose existence Theron had been hitherto unaware. When Theron goes to Father Forbes's home, in order to talk of his projected book on Abraham, the priest is even more disconcerting. "Abram," he tells Theron, was not a person at all but an eponym, literally, "exalted father"; practically all the names in Genesis chronologies are eponyms and

signify not individuals but tribes, sects, clans. And when
Theron asks if this is not a new theory, the priest shakes
his head and smiles:

> "Bless you, no! My dear sir, there is nothing new. Epicu-
> rus and Lucretius outlined the whole Darwinian theory
> more than two thousand years ago. As for this eponym
> thing, why Saint Augustine called attention to it fifteen
> hundred years ago. In his *De Civitate Dei*, he expressly says
> of these genealogical names, '*gentes non homines*'; that is,
> 'peoples, not persons.' It was as obvious to him—as much a
> commonplace of knowledge—as it was to Ezekiel eight
> hundred years before him."

Later in the novel he tells Theron that the most empty
and utterly baseless idea is that of human progress, for the
human race is still like a group of savages in a " 'dangerous
wood in the dark telling one another ghost stories around
the camp-fire' " —and this they call their "religions."

Man is a frightened wretch—half a savage—and there is
nothing new under the sun: those two ideas provide the
basis for everything that Father Forbes says. For Theron
with his belief in progress and individualism and his notion that Protestant American man was the final flower of
these processes and that the whole universe was ever creat-
ing itself anew with God smiling down upon it like the
sun streaming down through the leaves of the tree, these
ideas are profoundly unsettling. It is as if Father Forbes
kept pulling back the successive curtains that cover the
past, back and back through the abysses of time, and
always the same tableau: the savages around the campfire,
telling one another the same ghost stories. Thus the modern world that seems so new and unique is really a
ghost-world ever reenacting the primordial habits and
thought-patterns of the dead ancestors and continually
rebuilding the same structure on the ruins of the old one.
In Father Forbes's words: " 'Everything is built on the
ruins of something else. Just as the material earth is made
up of countless billions of dead men's bones, so the mental world is all alive with the ghosts of dead men's

thoughts and beliefs, the wraiths of dead races' faith and imaginings.' " With his two assumptions Father Forbes wipes out historical change and cultural differentiation and is thus the spokesman for neither America nor Europe nor even Western culture; he is rather the voice of an ancient wisdom which says that man is still a frightened primitive and needs watching. That this is so Theron finally realizes in his own person at his terrible denouement when he becomes, literally, the savage that Father Forbes tells him all men are. After Celia utters the crushing words, he thinks that he will kill her, and his mind reverts to the primitive state: it is in complete chaos but illumined by an "unearthly light,—red and abnormally evil. It was like that first devilish radiance ushering in Creation, of which the first-fruit was Cain." But the vestigial remains of his civilized consciousness tell him that they kill men who murder women. The rage passes, but he drops into something worse, into a pre-Creation loneliness and the silence of Pascal's interstellar spaces: "The world was all black again,—plunged in the Egyptian night which lay upon the face of the deep while the world was yet without form or void. He was alone on it,—alone among awful, planetary solitudes which crushed him."

At the polar extreme from this grim and timeless picture of man that Father Forbes draws, we have the brisk, good-humored, and contemporary outlook of Sister Soulsby. If Father Forbes regards men as potential savages, Sister Soulsby thinks of them as essentially good, although often misguided, boys. All he lacks, she tells Theron, is " '*sabe*—common sense,' " and Sister Soulsby will provide that ingredient for him. When he turns to her, after his reversion to Father Forbes's primordial campfire and to Pascal's space, now convinced that he is utterly depraved and doomed to die, she provides the necessary antidote, " 'as long as human life lasts, good, bad, and indifferent are all braided up together in every man's nature, and every woman's too. You weren't altogether good a year ago, any more than you're altogether bad now. . . . It's a see-saw with us all, Theron

Ware,—sometimes up; sometimes down. But nobody is rotten clear to the core.' "

Father Forbes, then, is the voice of history, of tragedy, of loneliness, of the unfathomable, of the mysteries that surround and encompass us, of our aboriginal fear of space and time, of the endless repetitions in which we are involved, of the point of view of "The Legend of the Grand Inquisitor"; while Sister Soulsby is the spokesman for the here-and-now, for life as a comedy, for the efficacy of common sense, for the sense of our common human solidarity, one linked to the other, for making do with what we have, no matter how insubstantial that equipment may be, for the point of view of *The Adventures of Huckleberry Finn*. As psychological surrogates for Theron they are unmistakable: Father Forbes is the "father," while Sister Soulsby is the "mother." Thus in the last analysis the two forces represented by Father Forbes and Sister Soulsby are not antithetical but complementary. There is no real argument between them and there cannot be, for both are right. Father Forbes tells us what we *are*; Sister Soulsby what we must *do*. What happens in *The Damnation of Theron Ware* is that the protagonist, having experienced in his own person the lesson of Father Forbes, turns instinctively to Sister Soulsby to pull him out of the prehistoric depths, which she does.

Father Forbes and Sister Soulsby never meet, but we may safely assume that if they did, they would immediately recognize and respect one another's position. Neither of them really cares what other people explicitly believe. Father Forbes's chief companions are the agnostic scientist Ledsmar and the symbolical Hellenist, Celia, and these two argue over possession of Father Forbes's intellect, a third point of view, and all three enjoy the argument. Sister Soulsby, in her wisdom, thinks all beliefs are nonsense. The only thing that the "Father" and the "Sister" disbelieve is the existence of Absolute Truths. Sister Soulsby thinks the truth of anything is bound up in its circumstances, and Father Forbes says to Theron in his last sentence in the book, " 'The truth is always relative,

Mr. Ware.'" Similarly they both value two things: intelligence and / or genuineness. Dr. Ledsmar, for example, after only a brief meeting with the Soulsbys is mightily impressed by them and speaks to Theron of their "genuineness." We may assume from this remark that the Soulsbys would have been welcomed by and could have held their own with the elite company of Father Forbes, Ledsmar, and Celia. The triangle, in other words, is complete, and it is mankind itself that is at the inverted apex.

6 WHAT SCOTT MEANT TO THE VICTORIANS

Will our posterity understand at least why he was once a luminary of the first magnitude, or wonder at their ancestors' hallucination about a mere will-o'the-wisp?—LESLIE STEPHEN, "Sir Walter Scott" (1871)

IN THE NINETEENTH CENTURY Scott was ubiquitous; in the twentieth he virtually disappears. Never before or since in Western culture has a writer been such a power in his own day and so negligible to posterity. All writers' reputations, including that of Shakespeare (with whom Scott was often compared favorably in his own day), undergo vicissitudes, but none can equal the meteoric rise and fall of Scott. In the analogy of the meteor, as it is commonly used, the stress is on the first part of the metaphor—the preternatural blaze of light in the sky. But Scott, more than any other writer, acted out the full, complete, and finished image. Now, in the limbo of forgotten writers, he still circles, an inert, lightless, mass—poetry, novels, editions, criticism, letters, histories, a life of Napoleon, mostly unread and unsung. He has even been dealt the cruelest blow of all, in that, although Scotsmen, professional and amateur, continue to revere his memory and, presumably, read his novels, he and his works have been dismissed and stigmatized as an anathema by the most vociferous and voluble of the modern Scottish nationalists, Hugh Macdiarmid. Macdiarmid, whose real name is Christopher Murray

Grieve, only grudgingly allows Scott one accomplishment in Scottish history—his issuing of the Swiftian "Letters of Malachi Malagrowther." Subsequent to 1825–26, the year of Scott's financial disaster, the English government concluded that the general financial decline had in part been due to the freedom with which private banks could issue currency. Accordingly, a law was proposed that private banks, both in England and in Scotland, should no longer have this privilege. As the measure would have worked considerable hardship on Scottish bankers, besides increasing English control over Scotland, there was an outburst of hostility in Scotland. Scott's letters were the single most influential protest, and the proposed measure was dropped. But Macdiarmid goes on to say that Scott was a "Tory of Tories, and a national liability rather than an asset in most respects." [1] In his autobiography, Macdiarmid singles out Scott (along with Burns for different reasons) as one of the real villains of Scottish history. Scott was Anglophile, bourgeois, a user of the English language (only the language of Dunbar is worthy of Scots), and a sentimentalizer of his race: "Scott's novels are the great source of the paralyzing ideology of defeatism in Scotland." [2] His only value, Macdiarmid argues, lay in his objective treatment of parts of Scottish history and in the fact that with the character of Redgauntlet he revealed his own suppressed longings in the direction of passionate Scottish nationalism; but he always remained a member of the "unionist clique" which had reduced Scotland to its present state.

Such was not the view, however, in the early nineteenth century, when Scott was not only the leading representative of his race and the great writer of his day but also what can only be described as an international force. If no other "great" writer ever disappeared so completely, no other writer before or after exerted such a profound influence upon the life of his times. Wherever one looks in the life and the letters of the nineteenth century, not only in England but in the Western world as a whole, one finds the impress of "the Wizard of the North." Then one begins to have an inkling of what a towering figure he was a century ago. He seemed in fact a wizard, and, as is often forgotten, he had not one career but two, first as a poet and then as a novelist. Keats remarked in a letter written in 1818 that in "our Time" there have been three literary kings: Scott, Byron, and the "Scotch novels." [3] The poet was the first figure to disappear and probably deservedly so. Wordsworth in his solemn and succinct way summed it up by saying that Scott's poetry could not possibly last since it never addressed itself to the "immortal" part of man.[4] The poems, then, caused only a few ripples, but the novels set up tidal waves.

It is impossible in the compass of an article to give full documentation and generalization to what Scott as a man, novelist, and historian-thinker meant in the nineteenth century—to the Scots, the English, the Irish, the Americans (both North and South), the French, the Germans, the Italians, the Spanish, and the Russians. I shall confine myself here to a discussion of what he meant to nine-teenth-century England, to the Victorians, and then only in his capacities as novelist and historian-thinker, leaving aside the man and the poet. Furthermore, I shall not point out his specific legacies to individual novelists, which are manifold, but will attempt only to give some sense of what the Waverley novels, as novels and as history, meant to the Victorian reader. There is a further limitation in that I shall by-pass—taking it for granted that the reader is familiar with them—the more celebrated Victorian pronouncements on Scott: Carlyle's and Lewes' deflations, Newman's and Ruskin's extravagant encomi-nums. Rather, I shall concentrate upon some lesser-known and, in my opinion, more meaningful analyses, especially those by Walter Bagehot, Leslie Stephen, and Nassau Senior. Nor shall I be much concerned with the immediate reception of the novels.[5]

Victorian criticism, not only of Scott but of most other matters, was half-way between—and a mixture of—Dr. Johnson and Coleridge; it was on the one hand judicious, concerned with analyzing and weighing faults and virtues, wrongs and rights, while on the other it was, under the influence of Coleridge, concerned with meaning. As for the judicious criticism of Scott, there was, and is, nothing new under the sun. Scott himself, and most of his readers, were fully aware of all his faults: the vapid hero and heroine, the often sloppy or bookish prose, the difficulty in getting a novel started, the careless improvisation of the plot, the repetitiousness, the historical mistakes and anachronisms, the evident haste of the whole operation. Almost everyone agreed that his early work was superior to his later and that his Scottish novels were more authentic than his medieval ones. Andrew Lang remarked that by the 1880's any tyro could get things going better than Scott. And after Scott's death George Eliot made the novel serious, James made it an art, and Joyce and others have made it a raid on the Absolute. To go from Joyce or James to Scott is like going from *King Lear* and *Hamlet* to *Faustus* and *The Jew of Malta*.

But the meaning of the Waverley novels to the Victorians is quite another matter. All his defects on his head, Scott was an original and powerful cultural and intellectual force. Like Wordsworth, to whom he was allied in many ways, he had put together a new combination and, like Wordsworth, he was a mover and shaker: the world would never be seen in quite the same way after the Waverley novels had been absorbed. Scott did not cause the American Civil War, as Mark Twain claimed; nevertheless, almost every steam-boat that pulled in to Hannibal bore the name of a Scott heroine. To have been alive and literate in the nineteenth century was to have been affected in some way by the Waverley novels.

The obvious appeals of the Waverley novels can easily be enumerated: their originality, their humor, the earthiness and quaintness of the Scottish dialogue, the individuality of the characters, the melodrama, the sentiment, the good spirits, the "sound" morality, the conventional love story and happy ending, the nature descriptions, the historical accounts, the thrilling battles, the intriguing mystery of the author—the splendid profusion of it all as the early Waverleys poured forth. Scott had put together a whole new amalgam of literary elements, unique in England and in Europe. Coleridge had foreseen much of this when he described to an unknown correspondent, in December 1811, the elements that had gone into Scott's poetry:

> But no insect was ever more like in the color of it's skin & juices to the Leaf it fed on, than Scott's Muse is to Scott himself—Habitually conversant with the antiquities of his country, & of all Europe during the ruder periods of Society, living as it were, in whatever is found in them imposing either to the Fancy or interesting to the Feelings, passionately fond of natural Scenery, abundant in local Anecdote, and besides learned in
>> *All the Antique Scrolls of Faery Land,*
>> *And all the thrilling Tales of Chivalry*
>> *Processions, Tournaments, Spells, Chivalry.*[6]

I wish to do two things in this essay: first, to point out the less readily apparent reasons why Scott should have appealed to the Victorians, and second, with the gift of hindsight, such as it is, and even at the cost of indulging in a little amateur sociological analysis, to speculate about the possible appeals that Scott had to nineteenth-century people, appeals of which they were probably not fully aware.

One of the least understandable appeals of Scott's novels is what was thought to be their great realism, of which, in the context of the conventional novel of the day (Austen, of course, excepted), they were prize examples. In 1853 Delacroix read Lermontov and Pushkin for the first time, and they brought back to his mind the initial response to Scott: "There is an extraordinary feeling of reality about them, the quality that took everybody by surprise in Sir Walter Scott's novels when they first appeared." [7] But in his own lifetime, and in consequence of his theories about the "advance" of art, Delacroix, who had once admired Scott and in fact had gone to England in the 1820's to study him and Byron and Hunt, came to admire him less and less as he grew older. By the 1850's he was complaining about the long-windedness and the over-abundance of detail in Scott's and Cooper's novels.

It is often forgotten that one of Scott's impulses in writing *Waverley* was the same one that initially set off Cervantes, Fielding, and Jane Austen—that is, to laugh off the stage the currently fashionable romances in the name of realism. Thus in the first chapter of *Waverley*, Scott announced what the novel could have been but was not, and ticked off the current fashions. He could have called it "Waverley: a Tale of Other Days," with a castle, an aged butler, owls shrieking, and so on; or "Waverley: A Romance from the German," with an evil Abbot, a tyrannous Duke, Rosicrucians, and so on; or "Waverley: A Sentimental Tale," with a heroine with "auburn hair"; or "Waverley: A Tale of the Times," concerned with the latest doings in the world of Fashion. His own object, he said, was to describe men rather than manners; to show those possessions common to men in all stages of society; to show the violence of "our ancestors"; and to take his leaves from "the great book of Nature." In the fifth chapter he paused to apologize to those readers "who take up novels merely for amusement," for going into so much detail about "old-fashioned politics," that is, Whig and Tory, Hanoverians and Jacobites, but his story would be unintelligible without this knowledge. His hero, however pallid he turns out to be, comes not out of the world of fiction and romance but is rooted in history itself by belonging to a historic family that had hereditarily fought for idealistic, and often losing, causes. The first Scottish village encountered in *Waverley* is a miserable cluster of mud huts, around which play children in a "primitive" state of nakedness. Their features were "rough," although Scott adds, like a good Scotsman, "remarkably intelligent." As it turns out, Rosa Bradwardine is the heroine with the "auburn hair," metaphorically speaking, but she is counterbalanced by Flora MacIvor, the strong woman and dedicated Jacobite. The whole Highland part had a ring of authenticity. Even Wordsworth, who was not lavish of praise, especially not for Scott, thought this aspect of

Waverley completely convincing. Moreover, the romantic and conventional plot of the hero and the two young ladies of his affections did not hang in the air but was embedded in, and dominated by, authentic history, by what had actually happened—the Jacobite uprising of 1745—and that not too long ago. (The original subtitle had been "'Tis fifty years since.") All the subsidiary Scottish characters were convincing and spoke a colorful, bizarre, funny, and seemingly realistic speech. Throughout his career Scott was always aware of the physicality of his characters, heroes and heroines excepted. The men tend to be burly and the women shapely, and one is always made aware, either by description or by action, of this great physical vitality. Finally, it was a world where people would fight at an instant and die for a cause. At the same time Scott's realism was not eighteenth-century realism with its descriptions of sexual peccadillos and its scatological references. There was none of the odor of "the bad century" in Scott's world, nothing that could not be read to the whole family.

A second original characteristic of the world of the Waverley novels was a great enlargement of the genre itself, temporally, spatially, and sociologically. Scott moved things back into the past but not into a past that was finished or irrelevant to contemporary concerns. Even the later medieval novels usually possessed a contemporary relevance. Similarly, great spatial panoramas began to appear in English fiction: the snow-covered mountains of northern Scotland in *A Legend of Montrose*; in *Old Mortality*, a castle tower commanding two immense panoramas: one wasted and dreary, the other cultivated and beautiful; then through the trees of the cultivated one comes a troop of soldiers, half-seen, half-hidden, winding their way to the castle; in *Rob Roy*, a huge lake in the northern Highlands. Finally, what had been predominantly a middle-class affair, the novel, Scott enlarged upwards to include nobility and royalty and downwards to include farmers, peasants, barbarians, and all the gradations of society, although, it should be said, the middle class always remained the real balance wheel and the center of gravity for all other classes.

At the same time, and over in the other direction, the Waverley novels were great compendiums of fact and information. Like a history book they had footnotes, and not only for historical facts but for general information as well. What did Glasgow Cathedral look like at the time of Rob Roy? How was a Highland hut built and what did the Highlanders use for fuel? Scott's novels were full of *things*: swords, armour, clothing, books, and so on. In *Rob Roy* before a dinner: "huge, smoking dishes, loaded with substantial fare, . . . cups, flagons, bottles, yea, barrels of liquor."

As no novels before, they pointed to and were allied with contemporary art and architecture. Historically, Scottish art had largely manifested itself in portraits, but after the advent of the Waverley novels pictures from Scottish history and legend became as popular as those based upon domestic and social incidents. Similarly, in the genre of landscape painting Scott fired the imaginations of his own and the next generation. William Allan, who had been helped by Scott's purchases of his work, was specifically influenced by Scott to turn to pictures of historical romance. David Wilkie too devoted himself, like Scott, to memorializing what was passing away.[8] Twice in his career, in 1818 and again in 1831, Turner himself was engaged to do illustrations for Scott's work. In 1831, Robert Cadell, Scott's publisher, suggested that Turner's pencil was needed to secure the success of an edition of Scott's collected poems. Without Turner, they could expect 3,000 subscribers, with him 8,000. In 1831 Turner visited Scotland, annoyed a lot of people, and made his sketches, twelve of which, as drawings, were exhibited in London in 1832.[9] Scott's appeal, then, was eminently pictorial, and his work and that of contemporary painters seemed to go hand in hand. J. G. Lockhart, early in his biography, referred to Pitt's quoting some lines of Scott's poetry and remarking: "This is the sort of thing which I might have expected in painting, but would never have fancied capable of being given in poetry." [10] Moreover, Scott's frequent references to Wilkie in the Waverley novels and his attempts to rival painting—he was in fact a frustrated painter himself—in his natural descriptions, with the resulting inference that prose and painting were analogous, were taken up later by Henry James and Proust and a whole generation of Western writers who conceived of writing, at least in part, in terms of painting.

In architecture Scott had a similar effect. Henry Russell-Hitchcock says that Scottish Baronial architecture was always "evocative" of Scott's novels and that associated with the Baronial style was a whole iconography of literary and patriotic figures: Scott's characters, kilts, tartans, Wilkie's Highland peasants, and Edwin Landseer's animals. And of course the two most famous Scottish Baronial homes were first, Abbotsford and, second, Balmoral. The rage for this architecture became so strong in Scotland that by the 1850's even the warehouses in Edinburgh were turreted.[11] Moreover, the same style finally permeated the architecture of the entire island. "The Scottish Baronial, combining the feudally romantic picturesqueness of the Castellated with the muddled Mannerist detail of the Jacobethan, was an almost perfect Early Victorian stylism" (Hitchcock, p. 284).

Other appeals of Scott are less readily obvious, but they were nevertheless real to the Victorians. Nassau Senior, who reviewed each of the Waverley novels as it appeared and later published abstracts of his reviews, is a case in point.[12] He had first read *Waverley* (author then anonymous) at a watering place. He was feeling dull and disgusted with the usual novel fare at his disposal, one item of which was *Waverley*. But any port in a storm: "So we opened it, at hazard, in the second volume, and instantly found ourselves, with as much surprise as Waverley himself, and with about the same effect, in the centre of the Chevalier's court" (p. 17).

Three years later Senior wrote that the Waverley series had grown to "a line of three and twenty volumes" (p. 8). This phenomenon was enough to alarm German diligence, and in English it constituted "the most striking literary phenomena of the age" (p. 1). Historically, said Senior, imaginative prose had been allied either to comedy and had given accurate and pleasing pictures of human nature, or to tragic romance, taking place in a remote Gothic past and falsifying human nature. Scott abolished this dichotomy and put together a completely original mixture of the two previously antithetical sides. He made the great familiar, and he made the past believable; his agents were the mighty of the earth, his subject the happiness of states. He managed to treat lofty subjects with a minuteness of detail, something that only Homer, Euripides, and Shakespeare had been able to do before. The legal background and trappings that Scott attached to so many of his novels gave them a great plausibility. For it was law that controlled and regulated the greater part of human actions. Scott's other subject, war, was ostensibly an interruption of the working of the law; yet, Senior goes on to say, in time of war, "the forms of law are never in more constant use. Men who would not rob or murder, will sequestrate and condemn" (p. 6). Dealing with battles, princes, lost causes, and so on, the Waverley novels were in the lofty regions of romance, yet, for the first time in fiction, these subjects were treated with telling and realistic detail, with the everyday facts of life always apparent: "we feel convinced that though the details presented to us never existed, yet they must resemble what really happened; and that while the leading persons and events are as remote from those of ordinary life as the inventions of Scuderi, the picture of human nature is as faithful as could have been given by Fielding or Le Sage" (p. 8). Added to this unique combination of romance and realism were other amalgams, principally the mingling of mirth and pathos in the mood and the alternation of the narrative and the dramatic in the mode. At times these admixtures were objectionable, but by and large it was all so admirably managed that it pleased both the reader who was partial to a particular mode and the one whose taste was universal. Senior was by no means uncritical of Scott, and he reiterated all the familiar criticisms: the often sloppy prose, the confused plots, the historical mistakes, the involved and tedious beginnings, the constant recreation, in book after book, of the same cast of characters.

Yet there was no Waverley novel without some merit, and in his best efforts there was always the joy of watching what the unknown author could or would do with a particularly demanding or difficult scene. Of the prison scene in *The Heart of Midlothian* (which he considered the most perfect, *Waverley* perhaps excepted, of the Waverley novels), Senior said, "we trembled for the author when we found he really meant to exhibit it" (p. 22). But Scott pulled it off perfectly. The trial itself was "striking" in its execution. On the other hand, the other famous scene in the novel, Jeannie's pleading with the Queen for her sister's life, Senior thought was not brought off to perfection because Jeannie's speeches were too rhetorical. In short, Senior, and other Victorian readers of Scott, were like spectators at a sport, watching everything with a practiced eye, or like gourmets savoring the choice bits of the feast.[13] Lockhart quotes a letter to Scott in 1818 in which his correspondent analyses *The Heart of Midlothian*: Scott had done what so many have tried to do and failed, namely to make the perfectly good character (Jeannie) the most interesting; he had by this feat enlisted the affections of the reader on the side of virtue ten times more than had Richardson. Admitting that she [Lady Louisa Stuart] was tired of Edinburgh lawyers and that the ending of *The Heart of Midlothian* was "lame" and "huddled," the lady correspondent continued with her catalogue of praise for dramatic high-points: the prison and the trial scenes were great; the end of Madge Wildfire was suitably "pathetic"; the meeting at Muschat's Cairn, "tremendous"; the characters of Dumbiedikes and Rory Bean "delightful"; the portrait of Argyll, whom she had heard much about in her youth, "to the very life"; Queen Caroline, "exactly right." [14] Likewise, Scott's new narrative techniques gained the admiration of people like Senior, who thought that the device in *Ivanhoe* of recounting the storming of the castle through the eyes and sensibility of Rebecca (through, in other words, a point of view) immeasurably enhanced the total effect by putting together such disparities as an actual battle and the wonder, horror, and anxiety of the persecuted maiden. But the real cause of Scott's success and triumph, according to Senior, was his ability to unite the most irreconcilable forms and the most opposite materials. This was his real distinction and originality.

If Scott was unique in some ways, he was familiar in others, most importantly in the ways in which his concerns coincided with those of Wordsworth. Wordsworth and Scott were the two single most important literary influences on the Victorians, and they overlapped, and reinforced one another, in three major ways. First, and most obvious, is the turn from city to country for background. The real revolt against the modern city begins here, at the opening of the nineteenth century, and the work of Scott and Wordsworth is its chief literary embodiment. The second way is in Scott and Wordsworth's ability to describe landscapes so effectively that they add a new dimension, in the imagination of the observer, to the landscape itself. Humphry House, admitting the difficulty of putting the phenomenon into words, says that Wordsworth gave the English people new spectacles after which they never saw their landscape again in quite the same way.[15] Similarly, nineteenth-century literature is filled with references to Scott's evocative powers. In his autobiography John Stuart Mill said that Scott could describe a landscape better than Wordsworth although he adds, realistically, that any second-rate landscape itself would do better than both. But more literary sensibilities were more deeply affected. In 1881 Henry James visited Scotland; he drove through a Scottish twilight, forded a river, drove up dim avenues to a great lighted castle. A certain Lady A put her "handsome" head out of a clock tower window: "I was in a Waverley novel." [16] In 1889 Lord Coleridge, the Lord Chief Justice of England, visited a rural region where Scott had never been—as Coleridge knew. But Scott had heard or read about the region and then described it in a novel. Coleridge was impressed with "the extraordinary fidelity with which Walter Scott had caught the air and general feeling of the place." [17] Visiting New Forest in 1900, Leslie Stephen remarked, "By crossing the road I get to the first scene in 'Ivanhoe'—the best beginning of a novel ever written, I think." [18]

A third way in which Scott and Wordsworth coincided was in their pictures of common life. Scott himself said repeatedly that he agreed with the Preface to the *Lyrical Ballads,* especially with its notion that, among the lowly, human passions received more strong and direct expression. This aspect of Scott's work and its similarity to that of Wordsworth was clearly seen by Keats in a letter written in 1818. He had been contrasting Scott and Smollett, to Smollett's disfavor: "Scott endeavors to throw so interesting and romantic a colouring into common and low characters as to give them a touch of the Sublime" (*Letters,* I, 199–200).

There were two other general concerns of Scott which helped to endear him to the later nineteenth century. First, the faint stirrings of feminism could be seen in the Waverley novels. The unconventional, almost pre-Meredithian heroine, was one of Scott's trademarks. These heroines were famous in the early nineteenth century, especially Diana (known popularly as "Di") Vernon of *Rob Roy* (one of the Mississippi riverboats was named after her), with her independence, intelligence, bravery, unconventionality, and continual protests against the inferior position of women. Scott's independent heroines seem innocuous now, but in their own day they were original and striking. Harriet Martineau, of course, seized on this aspect of the Waverley novels and claimed that Scott was a great feminist in both a negative and a positive way. Negatively, in his conventional heroines like Rosa of *Waverley,* he showed how frivolous, passionless, and uninteresting are unemancipated women. Postively, in Flora MacIvor, Di Vernon, and Jeannie Deans, he showed what a woman could be, if free, or partially free.[19]

Finally, although Scott was not particularly didactic

and although justice in his novels is not dealt out with the stern legalism of the Victorian novel proper, still the world of Waverley seemed to be under the aegis of the angels. Dean Stanley of Westminster venerated Scott all of his life. He called him "one of the great religious teachers of Scottish Christendom," and used to say "I am of the religion of Walter Scott." [20] Harriet Martineau claimed that Scott had "done more for the morals of our society" than all the divines and moral teachers of the century past and that his influence was "just beginning its course of a thousand years" (*Miscellanies*, 1, 30). She thought Scott was inimitable and that unless new channels for fiction were found, it would expire with him.

Nor was Scott's morality a simple affair. Noting the tact and sympathy—despite his own moral disapproval—of Scott's handling of Mary Stuart, Senior said that at last she had fallen into the hands of an author who deserved her, and went on to say in a discussion of *The Abbot* that in contemporary literature the rule of poetical justice was much too severe and unequivocal (pp. 61–62). Likewise, according to Senior, the character of Effie Deans in *The Heart of Midlothian* was exactly right—not too bad, not too good—for her fictitious misfortune; her crime too was precisely right (p. 22).

But the most complex and accurate description of Scott's morality is in Walter Bagehot's essay "The Waverley Novels." [21] According to Bagehot, Scott occupied in matters of morality a realistic position between two oversimplifications. The common oversimplifications were either to be "realistic" and to say that since there is no relationship between merit and award in life, there ought to be none in art, or—the opposite tendency—to be rigidly "moralistic," weigh exactly good and evil, and deal out exact justice to all characters. But life, says Bagehot, is not like either of these extremes, nor was Scott. Bagehot's summation of and answer to this complicated problem of morality in life and art is worth quoting at length. Scott's fictional world

is one subject to laws of retribution which, though not apparent at a superficial glance, are yet in steady and consistent operation, and will be quite sure to work their due effect, if time is only given to them. Sagacious men know that this is in its best aspect the condition of life. Certain of the ungodly may, notwithstanding the Psalmist, flourish even through life like the green bay tree; for providence (far differently from the real truth of things, as we may one day see it), works by a scheme of averages. Most people who ought to succeed, do succeed; most people who do fail, ought to fail. But there is no exact adjustment of "work" to merit; . . . "on the whole," "speaking generally," "looking at life as a whole," are the words in which we must describe the providential adjustment of visible good and evil to visible goodness and badness.

It is this comprehensive though inexact distribution of good and evil, which is suited to the novelist, and it is exactly this which Scott instinctively adopted.

(pp. 55–56)

In short, Scott's world was "real": "Good sense produces its effect, as well as good intuition; ability is valuable as well as virtue" (p. 56).

There are still other, more general ways of accounting for the Victorian love of the Waverley novels. Scotland was no longer the hereditary enemy and could be safely enjoyed as quaint and colorful. At the same time Scotland herself was, so to speak, conquering England— intellectually in the eighteenth century because of "the Athenian Age" in Edinburgh, and actually in the nineteenth century through Scott himself, Gladstone, the Mills, Carlyle, Ruskin, and all the other Scottish authors, intellectuals, and politicians who lived in England or visited there frequently and played a major role in Victorian culture and public life. The reaction against the French Revolution advanced Scott in many ways, the most important being the renewal of atavistic interest, in England and elsewhere, in the concrete complexities of history and race and culture. The Waverley novels were a monumental demonstration of the complexities, contradictions, and ironies of human (in this case Scottish) character and history. Fear of revolution was one of the great concerns of Victorian England, and here in the Scottish novels was a panorama of plots, uprisings, civil strife—but always put down in the name of the English crown. At the same time the underdog, the loser, in the Waverley novels was always colorful, sympathetic, inordinately brave, and, as such, was a literary symbol for all the underdogs in England, on the Continent, and in America. Thus, strangely, the Waverley novels became symptomatic in some minds of the aspirations for human freedom that were agitating the Western world in the nineteenth century. In Edinburgh itself on 1 April 1863, at a banquet for Lord Palmerston, George Douglas, the Eighth Duke of Argyll, made an impassioned speech for the cause of the American North against the American South in the Civil War. The speech was specifically aimed at Gladstone, whose complex sympathies at this time still lay with the South. All freedom, said Argyll, was earned with human blood. "Who are we, that we should speak of civil war as in no cases possible or permissible?" He conjured up the number of gory heads that had been nailed to public places in Edinburgh. And then he invoked one of Scott's martyrologists: "Do we not rather turn back to these pages of history with the loving chisel of Old Mortality, to refresh in our minds the recollection of their immortal names?" The speech was a great success—Gladstone himself called it strikingly eloquent—and Argyll received congratulatory letters from Whittier, Motley, and Henry Ward Beecher.[22]

Finally, in an even more general way the Victorians were longing for a national epic and got, for vicarious enjoyment anyway, a Scottish one. In the early nineteenth century the Western past was beginning to disappear at an ever-accelerating pace. Scott's novels constituted a vast memorial to part of that past.

It should be said also that the Victorian reaction to Scott was not invariably as clear cut or as serious as has been described above.[23] The Victorians certainly used novels as a kind of soporific or drug, the way mystery stories and television are used today, without any concern for quality. Burne-Jones, for example, read *The Antiquary* twenty-seven times and urged others to do the same.[24] Furthermore, many of the Victorians had a penchant for positively bad novels, to be enjoyed for their very ineptitude.[25] And the humor of Scott's obsession with the past was not overlooked either. On 11 September 1822, Sir Robert Peel wrote to Scott and, among other things, expressed his regret that the two were so far apart geographically. He wished Scott could visit him at Lulworth: "I can promise you a castle, two abbeys, besides a Roman camp and tumuli without end." [26]

Beside Scott the novelist, there was also Scott the historian-thinker. As an historian Scott and his work are best examined in three distinct but overlapping ways. First there is the factual and fictional historian who actually reconstructed the past in all its concrete variety. Second there is the conscious thinker, Hazlitt's wrong-headed reactionary, who knew all about the past and cared nothing for the future. Third, and most profoundly, there is the creator of the Waverley world with its various implicit comments on the nature of the past and the present and the relationship between them. At this level Scott himself was doubtless not conscious of the final implications for other men's minds of his own work. At this level too he is not just a simple reactionary either but a rather complex phenomenon, meaning different things to different people.

What immediately delighted his contemporaries was the concrete reconstruction of the past in all its multiplicity and color. Scott had been storing up historical lore for more than forty years. *Waverley* and those novels that followed so rapidly were like a dam bursting, as through these novels the past spilled out into the present. The Scottish reaction, of course, was nationalistic delight, and for the Scot these novels are full of nuances that the non-Scot could not perceive. W. P. Ker, for example, in discussing *Rob Roy,* makes something of the fact that it takes place in west Scotland. Though Scott was not a west Scotland man himself, he had caught all the distinctiveness of this type in the characters of Andrew Fairservice and Bailie Jarvie.[27]

But for the English, and Europeans and Americans generally, the interest lay in the fact that Scott had cut back under dynasties, dates, kings, and the abstractions of contemporary historians to present the flesh and blood of the past at all levels of society. If Macaulay did not approve of Scott the man, he immediately saw the value of the method of the Waverley novels for the historian. Macaulay's histories themselves would not have been what they were—he tried to make them as "interesting" as novels—had it not been for the Waverley novels. As H. J. C. Grierson says, Carlyle's *French Revolution* would not have been composed so vividly and dramatically were it not for the Waverleys. This side of Scott's work was summed up in Carlyle's famous statement: "He understood what history meant; this was his chief intellectual merit." [28] All this statement meant was that Scott, showing a past peopled by genuine human beings, made that past come alive again, a commonplace idea now but not so in the early nineteenth century. Actually, however, Scott's appeal was more complex than Carlyle's statement would indicate.

Senior pointed out that the early nineteenth century was precisely the time in human history when the "veil of high life" was being rent or torn away, when all men first began to feel themselves competent to scrutinize and judge kings and statesmen, considering them not demigods but men. The Waverley novels seemed to illustrate this fact. Furthermore, Scott's picture of history was dynamic rather than static, and his recreated past was peopled not only by concrete individuals but by historical forces as well: Anglo-Saxon vs. Norman; Scottish vs. English; Royalist vs. Puritan; Presbyterian vs. Catholic; the Past vs. the Present. Scott invariably chose for his novelistic background a crucial or seminal moment in history, a time when civilization itself was taking an irreversible direction. As Senior said about *Quentin Durward* (which had had the success in Paris that *Waverley* had had in Edinburgh): "Perhaps at no time did the future state of Europe depend more on the conduct of two individuals than when the crown of France and the coronet of Burgundy descended on Louis XI and Charles the Bold" (p. 145). Since then France has been a mainspring of European politics and Flanders merely an arena of combat.

But if history was complex and dynamic, it was also monolithic, resting on a vast communal experience that overstepped national boundaries. As Senior said, the fact that Scott was so popular in European countries with people whose historical memories were non-English and non-Scottish demonstrated that the novels were based on a "deep knowledge of the human character, and of the general feelings recognized by all" (p. 144). History was monolithic too in that, despite its complexity and ironies, it was all of a piece. According to Senior, once more, the Waverley novels showed how essential was national tranquility for individual happiness and what vice and misery follow civil strife. For always in Scott's world the public and the private intermingled, as they do in life itself.

Still, history was also process, change, and metamorphosis, and Scott showed this side of the matter as well. The feeling that nineteenth-century people had, that human nature itself had become softened and subtilized, more civilized and sophisticated than it had been in the past seems naïve enough now, after what has happened in the twentieth century. But this is the wisdom of hindsight. There was no real reason for anybody living in the nineteenth century, especially in England, to think otherwise. Thus George Eliot, in a letter to Alexander Main of 3 August 1871, expressed her annoyance at how people misunderstood *Romola* because they had not the historic empathy to see that Italian Renaissance man was a cruder person than modern man and therefore enjoyed very crude practical jokes which would offend moderns. She then invoked Scott: "I suppose that our beloved Walter Scott's imagination was under the influence of a like historical need when he represented the chase of the false herald in 'Quentin Durward' as a joke which made Louis XI and Charles of Burgundy laugh even to tears, and turned their new political amity into a genuine fellowship of buffoonery." [29]

It should be pointed out that Scott the historian did not go scot-free, even in his own day. Mistakes and anachronisms were always being pointed out. If it were a contest between accuracy and color, Scott would sacrifice accuracy immediately and happily. In *Old Mortality* he has a British regiment playing kettle drums as it marches through the wilds of Scotland at night. He was informed, of course, that regimental music was never played at night, but in subsequent editions he left the incident in for "the picturesque effect." Scott's Waterloo as an historian proper came when young John Stuart Mill dismembered his biography of Napoleon for the *Westminster Review* in 1828. In preparing to write Napoleon's life Scott ambitiously collected a lot of books and documents, but the actual research was hasty, sketchy, and superficial, as he was the first to admit. In his *Journal* for 22 December 1825, he said: "Superficial it must be"; but better be superficial than dull.[30] Scott prefaced his life of Napoleon with a sketch of the history and nature of the French Revolution, from his hostile point of view: "The feudal system of France, like that of the rest of Europe, had, in its original composition, all the germs of national freedom," [31] because everyone knew his place. Nature, said Scott, had always avoided equality: to try to erect a society along these lines was a "gross and ridiculous contradiction of the necessary progress of society" (*Napoleon*, 1, 69).

Mill had been reviewing regularly for the *Westminster Review*, but he rightly regarded his demolition of Scott as his masterpiece. He spoke of it in the *Autobiography* as a labor of love, for he was defending the Revolution against the "Tory" misrepresentations of Scott (throughout the review Mill calls him "sir Walter Scott"). His critique of Scott was twofold: the research was superficial and the outlook was provincial. "It is for sir Walter Scott to assert: *our* part must be to *prove*." [32] Burying Scott under a mountain of original sources, Mill said that Scott's point of view was the simple one "that whatever is English is best," and best for the whole world (p. 257). This parochialism made it impossible for Scott to understand that "mighty power, of which, but for the French Revolution, mankind perhaps would never have known the surpassing strength—that force which . . . converts a whole people into heroes . . . binds an entire nation as one man" (p. 255). Scott, the haphazard reader, and Scott, the simple Tory, were shown at their worst in this encounter. Scott's *Life of Napoleon* deservedly disappeared into limbo, but the Waverley novels did not.[33]

The picture of history in the Waverley novels is anything but simple-minded. On one level it constitutes a literary embodiment of Burke's principles. On 10 January 1831, Scott wrote to his friend Henry Francis Scott (no relative), an M. P., about the impending Reform Bill: "I am old enough to remember well a similar crisis. About 1792, when I was entering life, the admiration of the godlike system of the French Revolution was so rife, that only a few old-fashioned Jacobites and the like ventured to hint a preference for the land they lived in; or pretended to doubt that the new principles must be infused into our worn-out constitution. Burke appeared, and all the gibberish about the superior legislation of the French dissolved like an enchanted castle when the destined knight blows his horn before it." [34] Of course Burke did not dissolve all the claims for the principles of the French Revolution, as Mill attests. But Burke's position was not simple Toryism, and the link between the Scott of the Waverley novels and Burke now seems clear. And Burke was just one of several powerful voices in the late eighteenth and early nineteenth century—Dr. Johnson, Burke, and Scott were most commonly invoked—that spoke for the valid claims of the past. Mill himself was to recognize these claims in his later writings about Carlyle and Coleridge.

Even so decided a liberal as David Masson could see the validity of these claims. In his lecture on Scott at Edinburgh in 1859, Masson described what had happened to the nineteenth-century outlook and how this change had come about. The great dividing line in both life and literature was 1789. After that:

Our philosophy begins to deepen itself, affected partly by the deeper social questions which the French Revolution had forced on the attention of mankind, partly by the quiet diffusion among us, through such interpreters as Coleridge, of ideas taken from the rising philosophy of Germany. Our historical literature also takes on a different hue, and begins to be characterized, on the one hand, by more of that spirit of political innovation and aspiration after progress which belonged to the revolutionary epoch, and on the other, by a kind of reactionary regard for that past which the revolution misrepresented and maligned.[35]

There follows an interest in "the permanent and invariable facts of life" (rather than in "the changing aspect of human manners") and a "deeper reverence for nature" (Masson, p. 177). Wordsworth and Scott, then, were the literary representatives of this mode of thought.

This is all obvious; but there was a third Scott, a member of no particular party, and certainly not a simple and narrow-minded Tory, who is revealed not explicitly but implicitly in the construction and content of the Waverley novels. Going on the assumption that the proof of the pudding is in the eating, and that the complexity of a cultural organism is known by the multiplicity of its effects, I would cite once more the Victorian reaction to Scott, in all its variousness, as proof positive that the single-minded or simple-minded Scott in his own day was an argument of political opponents and, in ours, is a literary cliché. This variousness of appeal can be underlined by citing the passionate and lifelong love of Scott by such widely divergent temperaments and outlooks as those of Gladstone, Newman, Stephen, and Ruskin. By the same token, Scott's influence was equally various. By her own admission, it was Scott who first unsettled George Eliot's orthodoxy and started her on the way to agnosticism. But, according to Newman and others, it was Scott who helped to prepare the way for the Catholic revival. With the Brontës, on the other hand, Scott pointed in the direction of the wildest kind of romanticism.

Specific Victorian critiques of the intellectual freight of the Waverley novels reveal an equally complex reaction, which, already apparent in Nassau Senior's estimate of

Scott, can also be seen in the essays by Walter Bagehot and Leslie Stephen. Bagehot pointed out how impossible it was to classify Scott's works under the conventional rubrics; so far in history there had been two types of novels: the "ubiquitous," which is concerned with the life of man in its totality (of which *Don Quixote* would be an example), and, over at the other extreme and an invention of more modern times, the "love-story," wherein everything is concentrated on the fate of the hero and heroine. But Scott's work represents a transition in which the fate of the hero and heroine is attached to the life of man in the largest sense (pp. 38–40). Again Bagehot says that although Scott was a "romantic" and a "Tory," no one of any political persuasion could have given a more "statesman-like analysis, of the various causes which led to the momentary success, and to the speedy ruin, of the enterprise of Charles Edward," as described in *Waverley* (p. 45). Again, in the matter of the treatment of the poor in fiction, Bagehot said that novelists in general treated the poor in two opposed ways—either they catalogued their dreariness or made them into Arcadians. Scott did neither: "Almost alone among novelists Scott has given us a thorough, minute, life-like description of poor persons, which is at the same time pleasing and genial" (pp. 50–52). Bagehot should have added that Scott was describing a non-urban, non-industrialized poor.

This same instinctive sense to seize on a kind of *via media* between two unsatisfactory extremes was attributed by Leslie Stephen [36] to Scott's choice of the historical period in which he placed the Scottish novels like *Waverley* and *Redgauntlet*. In theory a novelist could treat any subject from the most contemporaneous to the most antique. But Stephen argued that either extreme was unsatisfactory. The present could only be viewed in a harsh, confusing glare, while the remote past was lost in darkness; and he admitted that most of Scott's medieval novels were false. The ideal time was the remembered past, where things could still be seen but not in a harsh light— "the twilight of history," as Stephen called it (p. 219).

And he said that all of Scott's best work could have been called, "Tales of a Grandfather." Everything that Scott was depicting was fast disappearing in his own day; he was thus keeping alive what was in fact dead, and his works are then a "vivification of history" (p. 220).

But, as Stephen went on to say, Scott was not only an antiquarian, for his "best service" was "not so much in showing the past as it was when it was present; but in showing us the past as it is really still present." His chief innovation was "his clear perception that the characters whom he loved so well and described so vividly were the products of a long historical evolution" (pp. 220–21). Fielding's lawyers imply nothing about lawyers in the seventeenth century or the sixteenth century, but "Scott can describe no character without assigning to it its place in the social organism which has been growing up since the earliest dawn of history" (p. 221). Scott was thus the first imaginative observer who saw how the national type of character is "the product of past history, and embodies all the great social forces by which it has slowly shaped itself" (p. 224). Although Stephen does not say so (and although it may well have been entirely unconscious on his part), what he very possibly has in mind—and he is writing in 1871, twelve years after the first publication of Darwin—is an analogy to the conclusion of *On the Origin of Species*, which closes on the precise point about the biological world that Stephen here makes about Scott's fictional world. In this celebrated passage Darwin called up the picture of a river bank with its incredibly complex myriad of life, animal and vegetable, everything radically unique, and yet all interrelated and made mutually dependent by general laws working so slowly that they could only be seen in the contrast between the present and "the earliest dawn of history."

Writing in 1858, before Darwin, Bagehot, in similar fashion, anticipated *On the Origin of Species*. One of Darwin's assertions that caused the most anguish and debate was that in the biological world there were no special creations and no freaks, as odd as many individual species may appear. Nothing had happened in isolation, and everything was under the simultaneous pressure of environment, time, and general laws. By an almost exact analogy Bagehot made the same point about Scott's more bizarre characters. In *Guy Mannering* Scott introduced one of the most outlandish of his creations, Meg Merrilies—a kind of queen among the gypsies, six feet tall, with wild eyes and locks like the snakes of Gorgon, "Beelzebub's post-mistress," "a harlot, thief, witch, and gypsy." Bagehot's point was that in any other novel such a character would be a freak, melodramatic and unbelievable, but that in Scott's world she is explained by her context. Scott showed how she "happened" in the same way that Darwin was to show how things in general "happened" (pp. 49–50). And in the Waverley novels generally it was shown how strange and eccentric characters developed naturally out of social norms.

This side of the Waverley world both Bagehot and Stephen took as a legitimate protest against the ideas behind the French Revolution. Stephen said that the radicals thought that what Scott, Wordsworth, and others stood for was a muddle of "sentimentalities." The Whigs, in their turn, thought the revolution would never extend beyond the Reform Bill of 1832. But in Scott, Wordsworth, and Coleridge, "Conservatism had its justification, and . . . good farseeing men might well look with alarm at changes whose far-reaching consequences cannot be estimated" (p. 224). Burke had denounced the abstractions and prescriptions of the French Revolution: "What Scott did afterwards was precisely to show the concrete instances, most vividly depicted, of the value and interest of a natural body of traditions" (p. 222). Bagehot made the same point and said that this essential assumption colored all of Scott's panoramas, from feudal society to modern Scotland: "the uniform and stereotyped rights of man— . . . would sweep away this entire picture, level prince and peasant in a common *égalité*—substitute a scientific rigidity for the irregular and picturesque growth of centuries,—replace abounding and genial life by a symmetrical but lifeless mechanism" (p. 48). The protests against the "symmetrical but lifeless mechanism" which today grow louder and louder were first uttered, or more importantly, first dramatized by Scott a century and a half ago, as Bagehot and Stephen saw.

But if anything, Scott's whole picture of history is even more profound and more disturbing than Bagehot and Stephen realized. For if Scott saw what was being lost with the march of progress, he saw too the inevitability of that progress. Perhaps the deepest insight into the nature of Scott's concept of history was that of Coleridge. In a letter on the Waverley novels, amidst many telling criticisms, Coleridge had this to say:

> the essential wisdom and happiness of the subject consists in this,—that the contest between the loyalists and their opponents can never be *obsolete*, for it is the contest between the two great moving principles of social humanity; religious adherence to the past and the ancient, the desire and admiration of permanence, on the one hand; and the passion for increase of knowledge, for truth, as the offering of reason—in short, the mighty instincts of *progression* and *free agency*, on the other. In all subjects of deep and lasting interest, you will detect a struggle between the opposites, two polar forces, both of which are alike necessary to human well being, and necessary each to the continued existence of the other.[37]

For the first time in literature Scott had dramatized the basic processes of modern history. Not that he believed in First Causes or Ultimate Ends—he was a sceptic intellectually and a stoic morally—or in a Single Explanation for the ways of history; but he perceived what in fact did happen in modern times. It was a struggle between the past and the future. But Scott's outlook was more complicated than that attributed to him by Bagehot and Stephen and more pessimistic than that attributed to him by Coleridge.

For Scott saw not only the value of the disappearing past, he saw also the inevitability and necessity of progress away from it. This is why—to the continuing indignation of present day Scottish nationalists—he always acquiesced in the final defeat of the colorful lost causes that he wrote about. At the same time he never lost sight of the value of what was being swept away in the onrush of progress, or of what can be called "the reason of the unreasonable," or the logic of completely irrational traditions. In *Guy Mannering* a certain Mr. Bertram is made a justice, an office which he has long coveted. Hitherto an inert, good-natured man, he is galvanized by his new dignity and rigorously applies the letter of the law. He ruthlessly commenced his magisterial reform at the expense of various established and superannuated pickers and stealers who had been his neighbors for half a century (although he also pursued and imprisoned criminals, for which he earned the applause of the bench and public credit). But all this good, said Scott, had its "rateable" proportion of evil. Similarly, in the figure of Edie Ochiltree, the beggar in *The Antiquary*, Scott gives a defense of the ancient and at one time honorable office of begging, and above all of the beggar's social function in his community: their genealogist, their newsman, their master of revels, their doctor at a pinch, or their divine. As for the economic status of the beggar, Scott points out that some of the licensed beggars around the University of Edinburgh in older times were supporting sons who were students at that same institution.[38]

It should not be inferred from this that Scott would have liked justices to be inert or beggary to be revived. He knew, and no one knows this better than a Scotsman, that modernity, with its impulse to control and to rationalize, and to organize all phases of human activity, was an irresistible, irreversible, and in a deep sense, necessary process. He saw too, unlike Coleridge, that the contest between the past and the future was unequal and quickly becoming ever more unequal. Lord Cockburn's memoirs— and he was a contemporary of Scott—are in a sense one long lament over the ever-accelerating disappearance of historic sites and beautiful natural vistas in and around Edinburgh. Similarly, the bleak determinism, heavy and historical, that was to mark later nineteenth-and twentieth-century Western culture in general had its real inception in the Waverley novels.

Scott's novels are peculiarly feckless at their center, that is, in the mind or sensibility of the hero, who invariably undergoes in his own person Coleridge's struggle and always comes out on the side of modernity. But while this eventuality is shown to be necessary and just, it never seems very exciting or colorful, nor is there any attempt to make it so.[39] This is why finally the Waverley novels come out for neither side—although Scott himself is consciously on the side of the modern—but merely dramatize the process in all its irony, that is, that the dictates of the intelligence are inimical to the urges of the instincts but that eventually and despite some mighty kickbacks and counter-revolutions on the part of the instincts, rationalization will finally control all of human life. As such, the Waverley novels constitute the first, faint, sometimes inchoate picture of an historical process that has become more and more in evidence since Scott's own time. In the twentieth century an entire literature has grown up around this problem, variously called "the rise of conformism," the "bureaucratization of human life," "the disappearance of individuality," and so on. It is a strange literature because while it points out an evil, it is not only at a loss to suggest any remedy, it cannot help but say that the cause of the evil is in fact a good because it seems to be the historical destiny of man to control his life and his environment by the exercise of his reason, which means, of course, conscious control and organization of all phases of human activity. Thus the Waverley novels are really in the mode of modern authors like Hannah Arendt or Roderick Seidenberg. The concluding paragraph of Seidenberg's *Posthistoric Man* could well be the epigraph for the Waverley novels:

> In the course of his development man has been constrained from time to time to abandon his most cherished myths. Thus he has abandoned his animism; his Ptolemaic astronomy that assured his position in the center of the

universe; his faith in a hereafter that endowed him with eternal life; his belief in the supreme and infinite worth of his person that assured him a position of isolate dignity in an otherwise meaningless and impersonal world; and even perhaps his faith in a God whose attributes, under the impact of man's rationalistic scrutiny, became ever more abstract until He vanished in the metaphysical concept of the Whole. The shedding of these inestimable illusions may be merely stages in his diminishing stature before he himself vanishes from the scene—lost in the icy fixity of his final state in a posthistoric age.[40]

But this is perhaps too simple; certainly Scott had a different perspective on the problem. In a letter to Maria Edgeworth on 4 February 1829, he offered a more problematical picture of the contest between the things that were and the things that were to come (the part of the letter quoted here was provoked by the notorious Burke murderers, ruffians who killed people in order to deliver the bodies to vivisectionists and anatomists—Burke himself was finally hanged):

> The state of high civilization to which we have arrived, is perhaps scarcely a national blessing, since, while the *few* are improved to the highest point, the *many* are in proportion tantalized and degraded, and the same nations display at the same time the very highest and the very lowest state in which the human race can exist in point of intellect. *Here* is a doctor who is able to take down the whole clock-work of the human frame, and may find in time some way of repairing and putting it together again; and *there* is Burke with the body of his murdered country-woman on his back, and her blood on his hands, asking his price from the learned carcass-butcher. After all, the golden age was the period for general happiness, when the earth gave its stores without labour, and the people existed only in the numbers which it could easily subsist; but this was too good to last. As our numbers grew, our wants multiplied—and here we are, contending with increasing difficulties by the force of repeated inventions. Whether we shall at last eat each other, as of yore, or whether the earth will get a flap with a comet's tail first, who but the reverend Mr. Irving will venture to pronounce?—[*Life of Scott,* v, 236]

Scott was quite correct in his intuition that for the masses of Scotland there was much brutality in store. By the mid-nineteenth century no other European cities could match the mass degradation of Scotland's industrial warrens. Frazier Hunt, an American, visited Glasgow in company with Sinclair Lewis and others in 1922. In his book *One American,* Hunt described his own impressions of, and Lewis' reaction to, the city.

It was a Saturday afternoon when we reached Glasgow. That night Red and I wandered off to the slums. I had seen Chicago's red-light district and New York's Bowery, and I had watched men have the D.T.'s on the streets of Brisbane, Australia. I had seen opium dens in Shanghai and tequila and *aguardiente* bars in Mexico, but never had I seen anything to compare with this Scotch border town at the hour when the pubs closed for the week end. Men, women, and children were fighting in the dirty streets; gin-drinking charwomen were lying helpless in the gutters and alleys; a quarter of a great city was over-run with hundreds of poor, helpless, drunken wretches whose only sin was poverty, and who for a few hours were finding escape from their everlasting fears and their defeats by the only road they knew.

Finally Red stopped and raised his clenched fists to high heaven. Tears were streaming down his cheeks. "I can't stand it any more," he cried. "I can't stand it!"

All the way back to the hotel he cursed and raved. "God damn the society that will permit such poverty! God damn the religions that stand for such a putrid system! God damn 'em all!" [41]

Still the past cannot withstand the future, though the two must remain enemies and though generations must be trod down in their contest. A growl from the past, such as Leslie Stephen's concluding sentence to his essay on Scott, "Those to come must take care of themselves" (p. 229), is endurable only if one can assent to Santayana's dictum: "The necessity of rejecting and destroying some things that are beautiful is the deepest curse of existence."

7   DICKENS
AND THE SENSE OF TIME

A DISCUSSION OF the sense of time in Dickens breaks down
into two categories: the concrete and the philosophical.
By concrete is meant such things as the historical date at
which he placed his imaginary events and the actual chronology of the novels. By philosophical is meant ideas or
concepts regarding the nature of time that appear or play
a role in the novels.

The concrete has already been admirably and authorita-
tively handled in Humphrey House's *The Dickens World*
and by Kathleen Tillotson in *Novels of the Eighteen-
Forties.*[1] As House points out, Dickens was rather haphazard about dating his novels, sometimes assigning them a
specific place in time and sometimes leaving the matter
vague. Both historical novels, *Barnaby Rudge* and *A Tale
of Two Cities,* are of course precisely dated and begin in
the same year, 1775. Of all the other novels only *The
Pickwick Papers* and *Little Dorrit* are given an exact place
in time, *Pickwick* 1827–31, and *Little Dorrit* in the middle
1820's. By climate of opinion and occurrence of historical
events, one can infer, as House demonstrates, the general
date of some of the others: *Oliver Twist* the late 'thirties;
Dombey and Son the 'forties; *Our Mutual Friend* the
'sixties; and *Edwin Drood* the 'fifties. With most of the
others, and in part with these, the events and ideas that
Dickens sets down side by side in a novel were in actuality
drawn from differing periods in the nineteenth century.
For example, while *Little Dorrit* is supposed to have occurred in the 'twenties, the attack on the Circumlocution

Office was inspired by the muddles over the Crimean War, an event of considerably later date in actual history. The historical events, the ideas, the social fabric of *Bleak House* are a conglomerate from such widely separated years that it is impossible to establish any specific historical time for the novel. If there were any principle working at all, it would appear that Dickens' instincts prompted him to use the memories of his own early years for background. In House's words:

> This continued habit of drawing on his own past is of the greatest importance to anybody who wants to treat Dickens's books as historical documents, or to see them in relation to their age; for it meant that he tended to push his stories back in time so that the imaginary date was a good deal earlier than the date of writing (p. 21).

On the other hand, the reformist elements usually were contemporaneous with the time of writing, as in the case of *Little Dorrit* already mentioned.

Mrs. Tillotson—although she would disagree with House about *Dombey*, which, she argues, takes place consistently in the present in which it was written—adds that not only Dickens but practically all the Victorians were retrospective in their outlook and had a tendency to push novelistic time back behind the 1830's to the pre-railway era (p. 107).

Chronology in the novels is likewise a haphazard affair. The historical novels, of course, are carefully and correctly dated. With some of the others, *Great Expectations* for example, the ages and the aging of characters is carefully done. But most of the time there is, as House says, only a kind of surface tidiness, and it would be impossible to work out an exact and detailed chronology for most of the novels. Once more Mrs. Tillotson would except *Martin Chuzzlewit* from this generalization, although she agrees with House that Dickens' time sense was "peculiar" (p. 110). It would appear simply that he did not care, nor do his readers, whether his "histories" (for he often thought of himself as an "historian") were exactly and precisely plotted and charted as regards chronology. Occasionally, one can see him make a start in this direction, but then, his creative frenzy upon him, he drops such prosaic matters for the more important ones of characters and events. The beginning of *Oliver Twist*, for example, represents a manful attempt to account for all things temporally. We know that at the age of nine Oliver is put into the main workhouse; after six months here, on a fatal day, he asks for "more"; he is a week in solitary confinement and is then sent to Sowerberrys; after three weeks to a month he is made a "mute"; after a month's trial he is apprenticed; walking to London, a distance of seventy miles, took him seven days; and so on. But when Oliver gets caught up with Fagin and his machinations, the plot time speeds up while chronological plotting ceases. So we are surprised, all of a sudden, to find that three years have passed somehow and that Oliver has become twelve years old.

As for a philosophical attitude toward temporality, there are in the novels two aspects, one relating to the author's specific statements on the subject and the other relating to plotting or mode of narration. Throughout the novels there are scattered, sententious, and more or less conventional statements about time. There is rather less of this in the earlier works and rather more of it in the later ones, beginning with *Dombey and Son*; and, in the later works, the mood becomes graver, as might be expected. Thus *Barnaby Rudge* contains the rather trite observation (apropos of Gabriel Varden, who is old but still hale and hearty) that time will be good to those who are good. By *Dombey and Son*, however, the mood has shifted to the inexorability of time:

> On the brow of Dombey, Time and his brother Care had set some marks, as on a tree that was to come down in good time—remorseless twins they are for striding through their human forests, notching as they go—while the countenance of Son [Little Paul] was crossed and recrossed with a Thousand little creases, which the same deceitful Time would take delight in smoothing out or wearing away with the flat part of his scythe, as a preparation of the surface for his deeper operation.[2]

In *Dombey* too Dickens begins to use great natural phenomena as symbols of time, in this case the sea. Thus he envelopes with foreboding the morning of the fatal wedding between Dombey and Edith:

> Dawn with its passionless blank face, steals shivering to the church. . . . Night crouches yet. . . . The steeple-clock . . . emerging from beneath another of the countless ripples in the tide of time that regularly roll and break on the eternal shore. . . . Hovering feebly round the church . . . dawn moans and weeps for its short reign (IX, 1).

This kind of symbolism is developed at length, and not very successfully, in connection with Little Paul's pathetic and early demise, and is used again as a preparation for "Cleopatra's" death. Near the end of the novel it is employed once more to give a fatalistic sense of the passing of time, as Dombey's firm goes down and as Florence and Walter Gay marry, go away, and return home again. In *Little Dorrit* time is the river, and it is again the river of death. In *Our Mutual Friend* time is a river once more, "stealing away by night, as all things steal away, by night and by day, so quietly yielding to the attraction of the loadstone rock of Eternity" (XXIV, 414). Elsewhere time is invoked as the ultimate sage, who knows all things; in *Little Dorrit*:

> Time shall show us. The post of honours and the post of shame . . . the travellers to all are on the great high road; but it has wonderful divergences, and only Time shall show us whither each traveller is bound (XIX, 219–20).

Occasionally the time sense becomes incorporated into one of the main themes of the novel and becomes thus an expression of that theme. In *Hard Times* the major theme is the mechanical nature of everything in the Coketown world, from the machinery, to the buildings, to the human beings, to the educational system itself. Accordingly time becomes mechanized as well: "Time went on in Coketown like its own machinery: so much material wrought up, so much fuel consumed" (XXV, 101). In the darker world of the later novels, time is generally fatality. *A Tale of Two Cities* is filled with the grim forebodings of destiny. This same kind of feeling of foreboding operates, on a nonhistorical and subjective level, in *Great Expectations*. Here Dickens expresses this sense by an elaborate analogy drawn from the Orient:

> In the Eastern story, the heavy slab that was to fall on the bed of state in the flush of conquest was slowly wrought out of the quarry, the tunnel for the rope to hold it in its place was slowly carried through leagues of rock. . . . So, in my case; all the work, near and afar, that tended to the end, had been accomplished; and in an instant the blow was struck, and the roof of my stronghold dropped upon me xxII, 363–64).

Yet if time is fate and the enemy, it is also the mother of growth and development, and the root characteristic that Dickens lends to Satis House is the stopping of the clocks which represent decay and death.

There is little if any in Dickens of the elaborate speculations on time that we associate with Sterne at one end of the scale, and with Proust, Joyce, and Mann, at the other. Only occasionally does he employ the notion of the psychological relativity of time, as, for example, in *Barnaby Rudge*, where he makes the point that time for Barnaby, the idiot, does not really exist, nor does it for the dazed John Willet, after the rioters have sacked the Maypole. Again, in *Hard Times*, he remarks on this relativity of time in relation to human growth:

> In some stages of his manufacture of the human fabric, the processes of Time are very rapid. Young Thomas and Sissy being both at such a stage of their working up, these changes were effected in a year or two; while Mr. Gradgrind himself seemed stationary in his course, and underwent no alteration (xxv, 103).

But these kinds of observations are rare.

There are, however, certain assumptions about temporal processes that underlie Dickens' plots; these reveal that the involved melodrama we associate with him is not merely a crude device calculated to thrill his audience, although it is that in part; but more, it represents a complex of serious attitudes toward a world moving through time. And in the first person narratives, like *David Copperfield* or *Great Expectations,* the idea of existence in time as a compound of memory and desire is added on to the temporal implications of the involved plotting.

As for the plot, Dickens is here his own best philosopher. It would appear that he thought of the intricate concatenation of events and peoples that provide the substance of his novels as an exemplification of an attitude toward human existence; and, in truth, most of the devices of what we think of as melodrama are not false to experience but are rather of the very essence of experience—only, in melodrama, simplified and heightened. The relief at the last-minute rescue that audiences feel in viewing a melodrama is merely a milder and more simplified version of the relief they must continually feel at the last-minute rescues in their own daily lives, which are a succession of entrapments. And the putting down of evil and the triumph of virtue is a spectacle that we all enjoy and even occasionally witness.

To return, one of the stock conventions of melodrama is the hidden connection between seemingly disparate peoples and events. Dr. Johnson's description of metaphysical poetry sums it up succinctly. Here again, in this area, truth is often stranger than fiction. As Dickens remarked in *Bleak House,* which contains one of his biggest and most complex plots, "What connexion can there have been between many people in the innumerable histories of this world, who, from opposite sides of great gulfs, have nevertheless, been very curiously brought together" (xvi, 226).[3] To this should be added two more observations about human destiny that receive expression in *Martin Chuzzlewit.* One is about the relationship between apparent time and real time, and about the geometric ratio of change; this is prefatory to shipping young Martin and Mark Tapley off to America:

Change begets Change. Nothing propagates so fast. If a man habituated to a narrow circle of cares and pleasures, out of which he seldom travels, step beyond it, though for never so brief a space, his departure from this monotonous scene on which he has been an actor of importance, would seem to be the signal for instant confusion. As if, in the gap he had left, the wedge of change were driven to the head, rending what was a solemn mass to fragments, things cemented and held together by the usages of the years, burst asunder in as many weeks. The mine which Time has slowly dug beneath familiar objects, is sprung in an instant; and what was rock before, becomes but sand and dust (VI, 363).

In this metaphor time is a mine, long in the laying but sudden to explode. The other figure that Dickens uses to describe time in *Martin Chuzzlewit* modifies this conception and gives us a third metaphysic of time. This is in relation to the death of old Anthony: "One new mound was there which had not been there last night. Time burrowing like a mole below the ground, had marked his track by throwing up another heap of earth. And that was all" (1,395).

These three notions about human relations, the idea of the hidden interrelatedness of seemingly disparate events which time will eventually unfold, the idea that change begets change in an explosive fashion with time as a mine, and the idea of time as a mole steadily working away underground constitute the metaphysic behind Dickens' plots. Each of these concepts implies a fairly basic attitude toward life. The idea of hidden connections assumes that there is an essential unity and binding character for experience; the idea about the explosive force of change implies that human affairs are basically anarchic and expansive in character; the idea of time as an inevitable mole assumes something different from either unity or anarchy; it merely says that there is a certain steady inevitability to all human experience and that things will be what they will be, irrespective of special events. Each of these principles operates in the novels, not as a conscious metaphysic, of course, and not to the exclusion of Dickens' primary interest in concocting a good plot. Seriously considered, they represent practically all the attitudes that one can have toward experience: it is a unity, or it is an anarchy, or, simply, it just happened.

In actual practice in a typical novel there are two plot lines. One consists of the surface events, change begetting change, in a world that is seemingly centrifugal in nature: things fly apart, lovers are separated, old men die, stocks crash, villainy is on high. But there are hints and shades of mysteries of which the reader does not know the full import: the poor little waif may be a prince in disguise; the mysterious stranger is actually the father of the heroine, and so on.[4] This submerged plot, that is not fully elucidated until the end, that is centripetal in nature, and that ties everything together, is the mole burrowing underground, or, to put it another way, the carefully planned mine which is suddenly exploded at the end. It should be added that the word "explosion" does not describe with any precision those interminable explanations that are sometimes given at the end of a Dickens novel, as in *Little Dorrit*.

The other temporal perspective that Dickens employed was first person narrative, which is superimposed upon the other two elements already mentioned. The gains from this device were considerable and much of the charm of the three novels where it is most extensively used—*David Copperfield, Bleak House,* and *Great Expectations*—is bound up with the fact that memory and desire (narration is both present time and retrospective) have been added to the unity and variety of the plot.

The least effective use of it is made in *Bleak House,* which is narrated partly by the pallid Esther Summerson and partly by the omniscient author. But while Esther is not exciting in herself, the point of view she represents—a person who has experienced the whole story beforehand and who, with the hindsight thus gained, can hint dimly at portents of the future and who by the power of memory can reconstruct the remote past—is valuable. Similarly and much more effectively, *Great Expectations* moves between the poles of presentiment and remembrance. The peculiar sadness of the story results in great part from the sense of fatality that is imparted by Pip to its narration; for, as in *Bleak House*, the real perspective, in spite of a continuous present, is retrospective. Thus when Estella insults the "coarse" little blacksmith boy and asks him why he does not cry, as he had so satisfactorily done before, Pip replies: " 'Because I'll never cry for you again,' said I. Which was, I suppose, as false a declaration as ever was made; for I was inwardly crying for her then, and I know what I know of the pain she cost me afterwards" (xxii, 94). Counterbalancing these bruitings of the future are reminiscences of the past, preeminently concerning Joe and the forge and the marshes and Satis House. Returning after a long absence to see Satis House, Miss Havisham, and Estella once more, Pip resumes his old occupation of pushing Miss Havisham around in her chair: "It was like pushing the chair itself back into the past, when we began the old slow circuit" (xxii, 277–78). Thus, although the narration is generally in the present tense, the plot is really suspended between the poles of the past and the future.

But the Dickens classic in the autobiographical mode is *David Copperfield*,[5] and in reading it, one almost seems to be recollecting one's own childhood, irrespective of the facts, so skillfully are the modes and habits of memory evoked, so accurately are the ways in which the world changes as one grows up described, and so powerfully wrought is the mood of the lonely young ego dreaming of the great universe and futurity. In some respects David's childhood is to him, as he says, a "blank." Yet certain things stand out, and rather ordinary things at that, as cataclysms. Betsy Trotwood's abrupt disappearance, for example, after hearing that Mrs. Copperfield has brought forth a boy rather than a girl, becomes in David's young memory, after he is later told of it, an event of enormous finality:

> Betsy Trotwood Copperfield was for ever in the land of dreams and shadows, the tremendous region whence I had so lately traveled; and the light upon the window of our

room shone out upon the earthly bourne of all such travell-
ers, and the mound above the ashes and the dust that once
was he, without whom I had never been (xiv, 19).

The novel captures likewise that peculiar sense of timeless-
ness that pervades certain periods of childhood with the
feeling that everything is going to go on forever in exactly
the same way it happens to be going on at present. Playing
with little Emily at Yarmouth, David has this feeling:
"The days sported by us, as if Time had not grown up
himself yet, but were a child too, and always at play . . .
we had no future. . . . We made no more provision for
growing older, than we did for growing younger" (xiv,
44). On the other hand, the propensity of the child in
difficulty to see time as a tortoise is dramatized as well,
and David's five-day incarceration by Murdstone seems to
occupy "the place of years in my remembrance" (xiv, 70).
Different still is the periodic sense of a tremendous
speed-up in temporal sequence during certain climactic
happenings. David experiences this at Dr. Creakle's; again
at Dr. Strong's, as he finally grows up, graduates, and
starts out on his own; and again during his courtship and
wedding, which is related in the present tense and is quite
different, in its abruptness, from the leisurely pace of the
rest of the narrative.

Less clearly defined but more important are what might
be called the temporal modes of the book, initiatory and
forward looking in boyhood, reminiscent and retrospective
in adulthood. The anticipatory quality of childhood is
perhaps best summed up in David's feelings when he goes
to his bedroom for the first night at Betsy Trotwood's:

> I still sat looking at the moonlight on the water, as if I
> could hope to read my fortune in it, as in a bright book; or
> to see my mother, with her child, coming from heaven.
> . . . I remember how I seemed to float, then, down the
> melancholy glory of that track upon the sea, away into the
> world of dreams (xiv, 238).

And the mood of the last part is precisely the opposite.
Looking at Steerforth's house once again, years after he
had first met its young master he reminisces,

> a long train of meditations . . . mingled with childish
> recollections and later fancies, the ghosts of half-formed
> hopes, the broken shadows of disappointments dimly seen
> and understood, the blending of experience and imagina-
> tion (xv, 277).

Throughout the whole book runs the perpetual dwindling of peoples and places, the sense of shrinkage that is one of the prices paid for maturity. Peggotty's cottage becomes smaller, the Murdstones lapse into ordinary and rather pathetic egotists, Dora becomes a silly little child and their marriage a rather foolish affair. Thus however shadowy, as a character, David may become in the latter part of the book, he is invaluable as a temporal perspective, and it is the temporal mood which he lends to the entire novel that provides much of its abiding charm and pathos.

Dickens, then, had two main temporal modes: the public plot—the mole burrowing or the mine exploding; and the subjective experience—the ego remembering. In full maturity he could bring both modes together, as in *David Copperfield* and *Great Expectations*. His own favorite of all his works was *David*, and one of the reasons for this liking, besides the autobiographical identification, certainly lay in the fact that it had brought out and given full exercise to these abiding temporal preoccupations.

THE LIFE OF THE LONDON POOR in the nineteenth century was, for the most part, miserable, and no one who has read Henry Mayhew, that great sociologist, can ever forget his grim and heartbreaking peoples and scenes. If man had set out consciously to fashion a hell for his fellow men, he could not have done better than nineteenth-century English culture did with the poor who "lived" off the streets of London. Indeed Mayhew's descriptions in *London Labour and the London Poor* sometimes convey a kind of Pandemonium quality and one can almost sniff the sulphur in the air. His description of a crowd entering a "Penny Gaff"—a kind of temporary theater which put on salacious performances—suggests some of the horror.

> Forward they came, bringing an overpowering stench with them, laughing and yelling as they pushed their way through the waiting room. One woman carrying a sickly child with a bulging forehead, was reeling drunk, the saliva running down her mouth as she stared about with a heavy fixed eye. Two boys were pushing her from side to side, while the poor infant slept, breathing heavily, as if stupified, through the din. Lads jumping on girls, and girls laughing hysterically from being tickled by the youths behind them, every one shouting and jumping, presented a mad scene of frightful enjoyment.[1]

But if anything, as over against this evil of stench and noise, the lonely pathos of individual tragedies is even more frightful: the blind street-seller who had once been a tailor and had worked in a room seven feet square, with six other people, from five in the morning until ten at night, the room having no chimney or window or fire, though no fire was needed even in the winter, and in the summer it was like an oven. This is what it was like in the daytime, but "no mortal tongue," the man told Mayhew, could describe what it was like at night when the two great gaslights went on. Many times the men had to be carried out of the room fainting for air. They told the master he was killing them, and they knew he had other rooms, but to no avail. The gaslights burned into the man's eyes and into his brain until, "at last, I was seized with rheumatics in the brain, and obliged to go into St. Thomas's Hospital. I was there eleven months, and *came out stone blind*"; or the crippled streetseller of nutmeg graters, who crawled, literally, out into the streets where he stayed from ten to six eking out his pitiful existence, six days a week. On wet days he would lie in bed, often without food. "Ah," he told Mayhew, "It *is* very miserable indeed lying in a bed all day, and in a lonely room, without perhaps a person to come near one—helpless as I am—and hear the rain beat against your windows, all that with nothing to put to your lips." Thus, if in what follows, the life of the poor is shown to have some moments of joy, these are, it is remembered, only oases in an illimitable desert of misery.

And since the Victorian moral "code"—if there were such a thing—will be subjected to equally large generalizations, these too should be qualified in advance. Victorian "morality" is a very complex affair. In the first place, what we call Victorian morality is only middle-class morality. Above and below, in the relatively small aristocracy and in the immense lower class, the puritanical code did not prevail; and indeed, in many respects, the aristocrats and the poor had more in common with one another, morally speaking, than either had with the middle class. Noting the passion for cardplaying, for example, that prevailed among aristocrats and commoners, Mayhew remarked, "It has been said that there is a close resemblance between many of the characteristics of a very high class, socially, and a very low class." Considering the life of the aristocracy as a whole, one cannot doubt but that life often ran high in those days, despite the decorous national examples of Victoria and Albert. Writing to Forster from Paris in 1856, Dickens relates an incident, given by a friend, of an experience with the English squirearchy. Dickens' friend, designated as "B," had, three years previously, been living near Gadshill and occupied himself with sketching in the outdoors. One day a gentleman stopped his carriage and invited "B" to come to his house and use his library. "B" accepted the invitation and stayed on at the house, as it turned out, for six months. The lady of the house aged twenty-five, was the squire's mistress. (He was married but separated from his wife.) The young lady, very beautiful, was engaged in drinking herself to death, while the squire, though "utterly depraved and wicked" was "an excellent scholar, an admirable linguist, and a great theologian." There were also two other "mad" visitors who stayed six months. Tea, coffee, even water, were seldom seen in this establishment: "Breakfast: leg of mutton, champagne, beer and brandy. Lunch: shoulder of mutton, champagne, beer and brandy. Dinner: every conceivable dish (Squire's income £7,000 — a year), champagne, beer and brandy." The squire's wife, in her turn, was bringing up their one daughter in vice and in linguistic depravity, in order to spite the squire. At thirteen the daughter was "coarse" in conversation and always drunk. At last the mistress died, after which the "party" broke up. The squire himself later died of a "broken heart." [2] And similar concatenations, minus the £7,000 a year and the brandy and champagne, were abundantly evident in the lower class.

As for the middle class, it is by now quite clear that the later nineteenth century and the early twentieth century had considerably overestimated the nature and extent of its prudery and of its innocence. In their private and personal lives there is considerable evidence that the Victorians were much less inhibited and conventional than we are, generally speaking, today. By this assertion I do not refer only to the obvious facts of George Eliot's liaison with Lewes, or Dickens' with Ellen Ternan, or the involved *ménage* of John Chapman or the *ménage à quatre* of the Thornton Hunts and the George Henry Lewes, or any of the extralegal sexual relations which any Victorian worth his or her salt seemed to get himself or herself involved with. I mean that the general *attitude* toward the private, "unsanctified" relation, while in theory it might be rigorous, often turned out to be in practice remarkably tolerant. Especially was there tolerance among the Unitarians and Radicals. Thus when Harriet Taylor, after the birth of her second child, felt depressed and uncertain, and uncongenial in her intellectual relation to her hearty, businessman husband, went to see her pastoral counselor, the Unitarian William Johnson Fox, the minister, instead of advocating fasting and prayer, determined that she should meet John Stuart Mill, an event which took place and has since become a part of recorded history. Coincidentally Fox, although married and a father, was the lover of Harriet's best friend, Eliza Flower. Later Mrs. Fox, finding her position difficult, made a formal complaint to Fox's congregation, and Fox had to defend himself in "open church." Mill and Harriet Taylor, whose father was a prominent Unitarian and whose influence was used, rushed to his defense—Mill believing him "innocent"—and Fox was vindicated. One wonders how successfully a minister in our enlightened and psychological age would weather a similar situation or if the elders of his church would rush to his defense if he were once accused.

Yet it is true that the middle class exercised a far-reaching and vigorous moral censorship upon its chief entertainment, fiction, although even in this area some qualifications and provisos must be made. First there were differing degrees of censorship in differing decades of the century. In the forties, for example, there was much less squeamishness than in the sixties, by which time the habit of family reading had become firmly established, and by the eighties and nineties Hardy, Moore, and others had broken the familial tyranny. Thus it was only for a relatively brief period, after mid-century, that the censorship was in full operation.[3] In the earlier decades neither *Wuthering Heights* nor *Jane Eyre*, filled as they are with an intense sexuality, roused any general furor on this score. Furthermore, even within the conventions and in any decade, the Victorian novelists usually managed to convey the intended effect. No one was in doubt as to what Becky Sharp was up to in her days on the Continent, after her fall. There is, too, in many of Dickens' novels a kind of implicit bawdiness—a jeering crowd of urchins or elders, with smirks on their faces and, one may well imagine, profanity in their mouths. Mr. Pickwick, for example, in the company of a young lady, is called by someone in the crowd an "old ram." Even in later decades, when the censorship was real and rigorous, implication could serve with great effectiveness to circumvent the code. Dorothea Brooke's marriage to Casaubon is both a spiritual and a physical tragedy. The spiritual tragedy is fully and explicitly analyzed, but the physical tragedy, while never directly commented upon by the authoress, is concretely underlined by the characters in the novel, particularly by the remarks of Celia and Mrs. Cadwallader. By them we are reminded, again and again, that the magnificent Dorothea, with her great brown eyes and her powerful maternal hands and her immense vitality, is giving herself to a dried-up old pedant with two white moles—with hairs in them—on his cheek, who makes unpleasant noises when eating his soup, and who has one foot in the grave, although, as Mrs. Cadwallader says, he evidently intends to pull it back.

Still, with all these provisos admitted, Victorian morality was stringent, and it exercised a stringent censorship on the novel, and, partially anyway, upon life itself. But its historical irony consists in the fact that it broke down, in the novel, if not in life, in the direction of the morality and mores of the lower class, whose conduct and attitude the middle-class Victorians found so reprehensible and whose "lapsed" and unregenerate mode of life the bourgeoisie attempted to meliorate, usually without success.

Mayhew reported that the costermongers said that tracts and sermons gave them "the 'orros," and, indeed, the poor were adamant in their unregeneracy in the face of the admonitions to "purity" that were administered to them. The classic instance in Victorian fiction is the impassioned retort of the workingman to the hectoring Mrs. Pardiggle in *Bleak House*: concluding a lengthy and aggressive list of his sins, he exclaims:

> How have I been conducting of myself? Why, I've been drunk for three days; and I'd a been drunk four, if I'd a had the money. Don't I never mean for to go to church? No, I don't never mean for to go to church. I shouldn't be expected there, if I did; the beadle's too genteel for me. And how did my wife get that black eye? Why, I giv' it her; and if she says I didn't, she's a Lie!

But the moral stance of the workingman, passive and helpless as he was in the context of the society of which he was more or less the creature, prevailed in a deep sense, and the revolt that occurred in English fiction in Butler and in Hardy and others, and later on preeminently in D. H. Lawrence, was in a sense an upsurge from below, an affirmation of the naturalistic and instinctive ways of life of the lower class, as against the theoretical and restrictive moral preconceptions of the middle class. And the history of the novel in the late nineteenth and early twentieth century is, in part, the story of how that workingman, whom Mrs. Pardiggle hectored, got up off the floor, and went, or perhaps staggered, to a writing desk, where he composed first *The Way of All Flesh* and *Jude the Obscure* and, later, such books as *The Rainbow, Women in Love,* and *The Man Who Died.*

The costermongers of the streets of London were without faith or hope, but, within the necessary limits, they practiced charity. They were, Mayhew tells us, scrupulously honest among themselves, although they could seldom indulge in the luxury of being honest with strangers. "Forgive us our trespasses, as we forgive them as trespass agin us," said a coster to Mayhew. "It's a very good thing, in coorse, but no costers can't do it." They were nevertheless surprisingly honest with the "deserving" rich. A certain Mrs. Chisholm, Mayhew reports, had let out at different times as much as £160,000 that had been entrusted to her for helping out the "lower orders," and the whole of this large amount had been returned, *"with the exception of £12."* They had no trust in banks or similar institutions, and although they had to pay usurious rates when forced to borrow from their own kind—sometimes at the rate of twenty percent per week, or no less than £1,040 a year for every £100 advanced—still their profound and unshakable distrust of all the institutions above them rendered them impervious to the whole idea of capitalism, investments, inheritances, and so on, although, it should be added, they passed on, like true entrepreneurs, the usurer's exorbitant rates to their benighted customers.

If the costers did not partake of the idea of capitalism that animated a great section of the middle class above them, neither did they bow down to the official Victorian deities of God, Home, and Country. Their nationalism was deep-grained in the sense that they disliked and distrusted foreigners—especially the omnipresent Irish whom they called the "Greeks"—yet they were completely skeptical, and rightly so, about the ecstatic chauvinism of part of the middle class. Like Matthew Arnold, they could be moved only to derisive laughter at Mr. Roebuck's Parliamentary encomiums on the beauties of being an Englishman in the nineteenth century. The popular song that was punctuated by the refrain, "Britons never shall be slaves," the costers rendered as "Britons always shall be slaves." For the detailed social structure of their society they had equal distrust and ignorance. To be sure, Queen Victoria's granite-like moral eminence was so towering that it cast a shade even over these lower depths. Yet the costers would not be solemn about Her Majesty, and mock love letters between her and Albert were hawked in the streets. Even her philoprogenitiveness was not sacred. The combined respect and irony in their attitude toward the Queen can be seen in the account of the "patterers," who hawked literature in the streets. They never, they told Mayhew,

had much to say about the Queen: "It wouldn't go down.
. . . In coorse nothing can be said against her, and nothing ought to, that's true enough." Yet one patterer, as it
turned out, had hawked "news" about the Queen during
her most recent confinement:

> I cried her *accouchement* [pronounced as in English with-
> out knowledge of French] of *three!* Lord love you, sir, it
> would have been no use crying *one;* peoples so used to that;
> but a Bobby came up and he stops me, and said it was some
> impudence about the Queen's *coachman!* Why look at it,
> says I, fat-head—I knew I was safe.

And the royal love affair seemed to have afforded them
infinite amusement. One street ballad, for example, had
one quatrain:

> *Here I am in rags*
> *From the land of All-dirt*
> *To marry England's Queen*
> *And my name is Prince Albert.*

Of other eminent people they were liable to have more
reserved opinions. The hero of Waterloo was not much
amiss, "if he lets politics alone," but the name of a bishop
was for them but another name for Beelzebub. The aristocrats in general they regarded as tricksters who somehow
got something for nothing, although they were completely
nonplussed, literally, by the concept of living without
working. As for the middle class, the patterers freely and
cynically exploited its prejudices, especially the anti-
Roman one. One experienced patterer told Mayhew that
although they peddled anti-Papal literature during religious crises, as in the affair of Cardinal Wiseman, they
had no feeling about the Pope one way or another: "We
goes to it as at an election." His own favorite, the man
said, was a ballad called "The Pope and Cardinal Wiseman" whose chorus ran thus:

> *Monks and Nuns and fools afloat,*
> *We'll have no bulls shoved down our throat,*
> *Cheer up and shout down with the Pope,*
> *And his bishop Cardinal Wiseman.*

The over-all politics of the costermongers was simple and direct: it consisted simply in a hatred of the police; in fact, said Mayhew, the police *were* their politics. They were interested in Chartism, and they were mostly all Chartists, although they knew nothing of the six points and they could not understand why the Chartist leaders exhorted them to peace and quietness when they could just as well fight it out with the police at once. "I am assured," said Mayhew, "that in case of a political riot, every 'coster' would seize his policeman." And among themselves they did carry on a continuous civil war with the "Peelers." To "serve out" a policeman was the bravest act and the highest office to which a coster could aspire. They were implacable in this pursuit, motivated as they were by a simple revenge code, and would patiently shadow a policeman for months until, catching him at a disadvantage, they would "do him in." The ensuing jail sentence was regarded as a mere bagatelle, and well worth the status of a hero among the costers that also followed.

If the costers had no concept of nationality or law or politics, they were likewise devoid of any religious sentiment or understanding. Only among the most miserable of the street people—the lame, the halt, the blind—could Mayhew find any religious notions. The blind musicians were "a far more deserving class than is usually supposed—this affliction seems to have chastened them and to have given a peculiar religious cast to their thoughts." But among the main body of costers only three in a hundred had even been inside a church or knew what was meant by Christianity. Occasionally a sort of Hardyesque feeling about the Deity emerged, as with an old sailor who told Mayhew that while there may have "once" been a God, He was either dead or grown old and diseased, for He obviously did not "fash" [trouble] himself with his creatures at all. But the bulk of the costers lived in cheerful ignorance of the facts of Christianity—"I don't know what the Pope is. Is he in any trade?"; "O, yes, I've heard of God; he made heaven and earth; I never heard of his making the sea; that's another thing, and you can best learn of that at Billingsgate"—and, moreover, out of the churches themselves they saw issuing forth only fashionable and well-dressed people. Although they hated the Irish, they respected the Catholic Church because they actually saw the Sisters of Charity caring for the sick. Protestantism meant mostly tracts and sermons and although they respected some of the inferior orders of the Church of England, Mayhew was told that if they were to join any religion it would be the Catholic. But by and large they were freethinkers. The patterers hawked on the streets—and this sometimes took courage—Hone's notorious parodies of the catechism and the litany, and after Hone's trial and acquittal, he had become with them a "hero." Especially were the patterers, who were the intellectuals among the costers, skeptical and atheistical. Some of them had actually had a classical education and thus had the knowledge to back up their scoffing: "Most of them," said Mayhew, "scoffed at the Bible, or perverted its passages." The patterers possessed a high degree of sophistication generally and were, in politics, "liberal Tories" who hated the Whigs and lamented the death of Peel.

But what troubled Mayhew the most about the costers was their imperfect concept and practice of marriage and home life, which the middle class had enshrined at the apex of its system of values. Only one tenth of the couples living together were married, and none of them had any notion of "legitimate" or "illegitimate" children. They thought of the marriage ceremony as constituting a waste of time and money, and the women of illegal unions were as faithful as those of legal ones. But none of them, married or not, had strict notions about fidelity, and in hard times it was considered no crime for a woman to depart from the path of virtue in order to provide for a fire or a meal. Desertions, heavy drinking, and the accompanying brutality were, of course, frequent, but it didn't seem to matter much. As one informant told Mayhew:

They sometimes take a little drop themselves, the women do, and get beaten by their husbands for it, and hardest beaten if the man's drunk himself. They're sometimes beaten for other things, too, or for nothing at all. But they seem to like the men better for their beating them. I never could make that out.

The whole idea of "home" was foreign to the costers. They worked in and often took their meals in the street. Leisure time was given over to the beer-shop, the dancing room, or the theater. The very word "home," according to Mayhew, was seldom used by them. The parent-child relation was likewise different from the one that prevailed in the middle class. Either it was established upon a nonauthoritarian basis: "The costermongers are kind to their children, perhaps in a rough way, and the women make regular pets of them very often." Or, conversely, it plainly recognized and made explicit the latent hostility which is part and parcel of that delicate relation. It was very common for the father and son to quarrel by the time the boy reached adolescence, and for the boy, who knew business thoroughly by that age, to leave home and set out on his own. One of Mayhew's informants said of the coster boys, "If the father vexes him or snubs him, he'll tell his father to go to h—l, and he and his gal will start on their own account." Adolescent marriages were common; two or three out of every one hundred boys of thirteen or fourteen were either married to or living with a girl, who was usually a couple of years older.

The patterers, as might be expected, were the least legalistic and the most irregular of all the street people as concerns marriage. As they were itinerants, they often practiced polygamy, and, like the legendary sailor, had a wife in every town. Mayhew had heard of one "renowned' patterer who was married to four women and "had lived in criminal intercourse with his own sister, and his own daughter by one of his wives."

Yet this way of life—dirty and precarious and amoral —had immense attractions, the first of which was absolute freedom. There were in the streets, usually among the patterers, well-educated people from the middle class who had chosen to drop from that class into street life. Mayhew tells of two brothers, street patterers, who were "well-educated" and "respectably connected" who "candidly" confessed that they preferred that kind of life to any other and would not leave it if they could, and Mayhew remarked, somewhat ruefully, that it was an anthropological fact, always and universally true, that no one in any culture who has adopted the nomadic way of life ever abandons it, while, on the other hand, as in Indian country, the reverse is often true and the "civilized" people will often become nomads. According to Mayhew, the nomads are always characterized by twelve distinct habitual attitudes: a repugnance to regular and continuous labor; a want of providence in storing up for the future; a power for enduring privation; an immoderate love of gaming; a love of "libidinous" dances; a love of witnessing the suffering of sentient creatures; a delight in warfare and perilous sport; a desire for vengeance; a looseness of notions about property; an absence of chastity among females and a general disregard for feminine virtue; and a vague sense of religion and a crude notion of the Creator.

Mayhew, of course, considered these as the stigmata of immorality, but, obviously, the costermongers were "immoral" only in a relative sense; and they had their own moral code, which was based not upon the sanctity of property and home—the basis for middle-class morality —but upon the sanctity of the instincts of the blood. Like modern psychologists, they were the enemies of "repression," and like the upper class they believed in the idea of the "duel." An article of their faith was that a fight should never be stopped, and when one broke out in the streets, a ring was formed in order to insure its continuance, "for they hold it a wrong thing to stop a battle, as it causes bad blood for life; whereas, if the lads fight it out they shake hands and forget all about it." Their social code in general was based upon personal feelings rather than legal or moral sanctions. They boasted of always sticking together, and a coster could always leave his stall, as a shopkeeper never could, unprotected, knowing that his fellow costers would keep an eye on it and see to it that nothing was stolen. Their own code was based mainly on the idea of personal bravery. This code dictated, for example, that pain should be borne in silence and with pluck. They were all pugilists, and a good one was a local hero. All the pubs had gloves at hand, and fifteen-minute bouts were the order of the day. Their sports were generally dangerous, requiring both courage and dexterity. "They prefer," said Mayhew, "if crossing a bridge, to climb over the parapet, and walk along on the stone coping."

Above all there was no place in the code for the middle-class idea of "respectability." Indeed the more intelligent of the patterers mocked at the whole concept. And the impudence and wit that Dickens put at the disposal of the "Artful Dodger," especially in the trial scene when he directly confronts the forces of law and order, were evidently commonplace among the costers. Although most of them were completely uneducated—only one in ten was able to read—they were preternaturally acute, for only by their wits could they exist. One of the quickest-witted of the patterers was interviewed by Mayhew and recounted an experience that paralleled, with a happier ending, that of the Artful Dodger:

> I was once before Alderman Kelley, when he was Lord Mayor, charged with obstructing, or some humbug. "What are you my man," he says quietly, and like a gentleman. "In the same line as yourself, my lord," says I. "How's that?" says he. "I'm a paper-worker for my living, my lord," says I. I was soon discharged and there was such fun and laughing, that if I'd a few slums in my pocket, I believe I could have sold them all in the justice-room.

And the great heavy Victorian morality overhead, which at its best produced such titans as John Stuart Mill, George Eliot, and Matthew Arnold, but which also produced, in lesser vessels, Theobald and Christina Pontifex, finally toppled over in the direction of lower-class morality, and *The Way of All Flesh* celebrates a way of life not far different from the life of the costers.

It hardly needs to be pointed out that Butler's attack

upon official Victorian morality jibes, almost point by point, with the actual morality of the lower orders: freedom, or neglect, for children, an early exodus from the parental domain, no tie to formal religion or formal education, impudence, in general, about the sacred cows of the middle class, a wholesale rejection of the idea of "respectability," an over-all anarchism, and a belief in the instincts. Add a private income, some book learning, some notions—none too formal or precise—about a Deity, and subtract the love of brutality and the terrible suffering that often prevailed, and a street patterer would come close to being a Butlerian hero. It is no accident that Butler has his hero shed his last illusions about the middle-class outlook among the London poor (whom he is supposedly "converting" but who in actuality convert him) and that after his ultimate "fall"—the period spent in jail—he should, like a street patterer, have dropped out of his own class and joined the lower one. But the heart of the matter goes deeper than explicit ideas and institutions. What Butler was attacking, above all, was middle-class consciousness, that is, the way the middle-class mind operated, and he opposed this consciousness with another type or way of handling experience, which he associated with either the aristocracy or the lower class, for it was only these that had the famous Butlerian "grace," the ability to act by instinct and by the unconscious. Towneley, upperclass, and Mr. Shaw, the tinker of the lower-class, both have this faculty because they have not been brought up in what was for Butler the prison house of abstract moral codes and formulations and surrounded by all kinds of taboos and bugaboos which attempted anyway to repress instinct completely and to regulate all human conduct— even human thought—by acquired precepts. Butler thought that St. Paul was the real villain in Western history, for he represented formulated law.

If Butler embodies the comedy of this revolt against middle-class consciousness, Hardy embodies in his career as a whole, first, its antitype as pastoral and, second and finally, its antitype as tragedy. The world of *Far from the*

Madding Crowd or *The Woodlanders* is the idyll from which, with some exceptions, the bugaboo of consciousness is absent, and where time has stopped and nature is benignly soft. There was a Hardy "mood," which all his admirers loved and which has no parallel in English literature. D. H. Lawrence, perhaps the best and most perceptive critic of Hardy, summed it up in a letter written in 1918 from a cottage in Berkshire: "It is very nice here—Hardy country—like *Woodlanders*—all woods and hazel copses, and tiny little villages, under the church, with fields slanting down, and a hazel copse almost touching the little garden wall." [4] Hardy himself described Little Hintock, the locale of *The Woodlanders*, as "one of those sequestered spots outside the gates of the world where may usually be found more meditation than action, and more passivity than meditation; where reasoning proceeds on narrow premises, and results in inferences wildly imaginative." Marty South and Giles Winterbourne, the real if not the titular hero and heroine, are Arcadian primitives, taciturn, in tune with the natural world—whose symbols they can decipher like hieroglyphs—instinctive, and personal: "Her [Marty's] face had the usual fullness of expression which is developed by the life of solitude. Where the eyes of the multitude beat like waves upon a countenance they seem to wear away individuality." Despite their mutual tragedy and Giles's death, they are outside the hell of consciousness. But as Hardy's career went on, the rustics got, in Henry James's phrase, squeezed into their "horrid age," with its formulations and conceptualized taboos. Tess is described as being surrounded by a host of "moral hobgoblins," false and contrary to her instincts, that harass her waking life and hound her to her death. Lawrence said that in Hardy none of the central characters ever really care about position or money or even immediate self-preservation. They are all struggling for that most passionate and most unself-conscious of relationships—love. They thus "explode out of convention" [5] and are destroyed, while those who remain safely and pallidly within the pale are saved. Critics of Hardy complained that his characters were always behaving in unexpected fashion and doing unexpected things, but that was just the point, according to Lawrence: they were acting instinctively in a world where the instinctive was no longer allowable. In Hardy, as in Butler, the burden of consciousness and the legacy of St. Paul have become intolerable, and in Jude's terrible death and in Ernest Pontifex's final isolation, we see two prophecies as to its ultimate end-point: either it will drive people to their death or it will drive them into outlawry, however polite and genteel, as was Ernest's.

But Hardy and Butler, while in some respects they point in the same direction, are in other respects radically divergent. Butler quite clearly looks forward to E. M. Forster and D. H. Lawrence, with their instinctive ethic, their dynamic, purposive concepts of life, their disdain for and lack of concern with the minutiae of individual consciousness, and their sense of comedy. Hardy, on the other hand, while he has deep affinities with Lawrence, especially as the poet of nature and the apostle of the instincts, looks toward the stasis and tragedy, the entrapment of the individual in the hell of his consciousness, that is the province of the later James, of Conrad, of Woolf, of Joyce. The one tradition looks forward to *The Man Who Died*; the other to *Finnegans Wake*. Thus Lawrence and Joyce, the two indisputably great English novelists of the twentieth century, in whose "wake" the novel still wallows, are not so much the unique children of the twentieth century as they are the grandchildren of the nineteenth, the twin inheritors and summarizers of the great Victorian novel, which broke, split, and diverged in two directions in the late nineteenth century.

It all began with George Eliot; at least this is what D. H. Lawrence thought. As young readers, he and "E.T." were both wholehearted admirers of George Eliot, especially of *The Mill on the Floss*. Yet Lawrence has some reservations as to the direction, namely, the psychological, to which George Eliot's novels first pointed. "You see, it was really George Eliot who started it all," Lawrence was saying in that deliberate way he had of speaking when he was trying to work something out in his own mind. "And how wild they were with her for doing it. It was she who started putting all the action inside. Before, you know, with Fielding and the others, it had been outside. Now I wonder which is right?" [6] "E.T." promptly replied that of course George Eliot was right, but Lawrence demurred, if ever so slightly, "You know I can't help thinking there ought to be a bit of both." [7] For he faintly suspected then what he was to assert so vehemently later, namely, that the exploration of the minutiae of consciousness was finally, magnificent a subject though it might be, a cul-de-sac, as it has since proved to be. This is what he meant by his later and more famous statement that he was no longer interested in individuals and what he meant when he emitted one of his characteristic screeches at most modern novels: "They're all little Jesuses in their own eyes, and their 'purpose' is to prove it. Oh Lord! *Lord Jim! Sylvestre Bonnard! If Winter Comes! Main Street! Ulysses! Pan!* They are all pathetic or sympathetic or antipathetic little Jesuses *accomplis* or *manqués*." [8] It is a rebellion against the intolerable "I," "I," "I," which is the signature of so many twentieth-century novels.

This subjective line that began with George Eliot and led to Henry James, to Conrad, to Virginia Woolf, to culminate in Joyce has certain marked characteristics both in content and form. Its content is the data of middle-class consciousness, usually described directly by the so-called stream of consciousness, or a variant thereof, with the exception of Conrad where narration is objection. Life is conceived of as static—nothing can change and nothing can really happen—and, with the exception of Joyce, tragic. But even in Joyce the major assumption is that we all are trapped in our own solitary cells, endlessly chewing the cud of moment-by-moment experience, slowly and sadly in James, abruptly and ironically in Conrad, poetically and wistfully in Virginia Woolf, rapidly and humorously in Joyce. The stasis, or entrapment, tragic in James and Conrad and Hardy, becomes wistful in Woolf and

funny in Joyce. *Ulysses* leaves its hero in a perfect equilib-
rium—nothing ventured, nothing gained. When Leopold
Bloom finally kisses the adulterous rump of which he is
the adorer and falls off to sleep, dreaming of Sinbad the
Sailor, he is certainly one of the most equanimous protagonists in all fiction, simply because he has accepted utterly
the fact that life is what it is and nothing can be done.
But the basic attitude of this genre is deeply pessimistic.
Space is imprisonment, time a tyranny, and history a
nightmare from which nobody can awake. The temporal is
an obsession dominating all phases of life. Similarly the
tone is nondidactic and seeks merely to describe, with no
moral or lesson or thesis. Once more Joyce is the culmination and fullest expression of the genre, and *Ulysses* is the
most scrupulously nonkinetic of novels. It moves to nothing but sheer contemplation, which was the author's primary and sole objective.

There are also formal resemblances in the Joyce tradition that set it off from the Butler-Forster-Lawrence line.
Primarily the tradition is self-consciously "literary," both
in structure and style. James, Conrad, Virginia Woolf,
Joyce, whatever their great differences, were all united in a
devotion to the carefully planned structure, from James's
"point of view," through the looping narrative of Conrad
and the artfully planned one of Virginia Woolf, to the
gigantic battleship, with everything in place from the
underwater bolts to the railing on the conning tower, of
Ulysses. Likewise these authors were all magicians of "the
word," not only the right words, but the right words in the
right order. For each, language per se was a kind of
daemon, almost an objective entity—a lovely goddess appearing to the breathless aging bachelor Henry James on a
New Year's Eve, a divine instrument to Joyce for trans-
forming that reality behind which existed a God in whom
he still believed but could no longer serve.

None of these writers was connected to one another by
any conscious lines of influence, with the exception of
Virginia Woolf's recognizing the importance of *Ulysses*
for the method and purpose of her own work. James was

"The Master," *sui generis*; Conrad a foreigner working in a strange tongue; Virginia Woolf all alone in her room with a view; Joyce an Irishman living on the Continent and consciously disdainful of all that had preceded him in English fiction. Thus each thought of himself or herself as a new start, novelistically speaking. Seen in retrospect, they all prove to be culminative and evolutionary, but this evolution resulted from the workings of the *Zeitgeist* and not from the workings of their own minds, each of which saw itself as unique, precarious, and isolated.

The Butler-Forster-Lawrence tradition explicitly reverses all of these characteristics. In the first place it is quite consciously interdependent. Both Forster and Lawrence were admirers of Butler and his intellectual unconventionality. Forster once contemplated a book on Butler, and his own novels are filled with Butlerian echoes and attitudes. *The Longest Journey* is a repetition of the Butlerian thesis that the intellect is not supreme and that only common sense and instinct can make existence bearable, indeed liveable. Lawrence and Forster, of course, knew each other, and although Lawrence, as was his custom, was sparing in his praise of Forster's work, the tie between the two writers is manifest. Forster's admiration for Lawrence's work and his recognition of Lawrence's genius are specifically documented in *Aspects of the Novel*, where Lawrence is called the one indisputable "prophet" among modern writers. And the "natural man" who figures in Forster's early work, either an Italian like Gino or an Englishman like Stephen Wonham, anticipate Lawrence's "dark gamekeeper."

The Butler-Forster-Lawrence tradition likewise has its own form and content. Formally, it prides itself on being nonliterary, without involved manipulation of structure or scrupulously maintained "points of view" and without agonies over the *mot juste*. Forster thought that the sanctity of the device of the point of view, made into a holy of holies by James and Percy Lubbock, was an artificial shibboleth and very consciously in his own novels he violated it. Lawrence's disdain for the artifices of art was notorious.

Whereas Joyce's method of rewriting was to complicate and complicate further, ever adding to a formal and precise structure, Lawrence's was to throw away the existing document and rewrite the original idea all over again.

In matters of content the Lawrencian tradition is equally divergent from the Joyce tradition. Stasis is replaced by dynamics, tragedy by comedy, and pessimism by hope. Space becomes freedom, time becomes growth, and history can be shed as the snake sheds its skin. Thus against the ending of *Ulysses* and its static entrapment, with Mr. Bloom accepting this entrapment, one can contrast the ending of *The Rainbow* where amid the thunder of the dark horses on the ground and under the splendor of the great rainbow in the sky, Ursula Brangwen sheds her own past and, by proxy, the past of her fellow human beings. This is a world which is organic and purposive; it is expressive of the anti-Darwinian argument that Butler had initiated, and Shaw had furthered. Studying botany Ursula rejects, solely on the basis of her own intuition, the mechanistic "purpose-less-ness" explanation of natural phenomenon that her professors give her, for she believes, against all reason and science, that everything has a "soul," even objects of nature, such as flowers. In her mind everything in the universe is potentially living and eternal, and time itself is no longer tyrannous. The earthly institution that most fully symbolized the victory over time of this Butlerian or Lamarckian universe was the medieval cathedral. Lincoln Cathedral in *The Rainbow* is described as:

> Away from time, always outside of time! Between east and west, between dawn and sunset, the Church lay like a seed in silence, dark before germination, silenced after death . . . potential with all the noise and transition of life, the cathedral remained hushed, a great involved seed. . . . Spanned round with the rainbow, the jewelled gloom folded music upon silence, light upon darkness, fecundity upon death.

Other institutions, such as the great country house of Breadalby, that symbolize the dead and finished past but that still, anomalously, survive in the present are described as snares and delusions: "What a snare and a delusion, this beauty of static things."

Finally the Lawrencian tradition is avowedly, one might say frantically, kinetic; it has a "message," and the burden of this message, from Butler to Lawrence, is that the middle-class consciousness has become thin and neurotic, divorced from primal needs and instincts. According to Lawrence the middle class is "broad and shallow and passionless. Quite passionless. At best they substitute affection, which is the great middle-class positive emotion." [9] A corollary of this distaste for middle-class consciousness, which had been developed by a restrictive and absolutistic morality, was a distaste for all absolutes. Everything in the world is relative to everything else, and nothing had any value except insofar as it is related to the instincts—Butler's "grace" and Lawrence's "dark power."

What Lawrence represents, then, is the culmination in the novel of that upsurge from below which the "ethic" of the London proletariat had prefigured and which Butler had first embodied in the novel. Without getting into the argument between T. S. Eliot and F. R. Leavis about the "cultural resources" of Lawrence, it can certainly be said that he was, definitively and defiantly, of the lower class rather than of the middle class. There can be no doubt that if the bawdy, bearded, dying Lawrence of the later years were to rewrite *Sons and Lovers*, the scale of values would have been considerably altered, if not actually reversed, with the drunken, vulgarian, dominated father emerging as superior to the prim, powerfully-willed mother, and Paul becoming explicitly the priggish soul-mongerer, the "little Jesus," that he implicitly is in the novel itself. By the time he hit upon his true province, the world of *Women in Love* and *The Rainbow*, Lawrence had come to realize this himself. Completely unsatisfied with Skrebensky, the preeminent incarnation of the middle-class consciousness, Ursula Brangwen imagines that there must be another kind of consciousness, analogous to that of the workingman: "It doesn't matter. But a sort of strong understanding, in some men, and then a dignity, a directness, something unquestioned that there is in working men, and then a jolly, reckless passionateness that you see—a man who could really let go—."

Joyce, then, represents the novel of middle-class consciousness in culmination and *in extremis,* and Lawrence represents the counterattack from below. The question remains: where does the novel go from here? For certainly it has remained substantially in the doldrums since the deaths of Lawrence and Joyce. Good second-rank practitioners are of course abundant, but major talents, such as came in profusion from the 1830's to the 1920's, are indubitably lacking.

It is possible, of course, that the big novel is a thing of the past, a child of the special conditions of the nineteenth century. Even the writers whom one would tend to regard as the products of twentieth century, if only for chronological reasons, such as Proust, Mann, and Joyce, tend to look more and more, what with their preoccupation with ideas, their minute psychologizing, their grandiose architecture, like legacies of the nineteenth century and culminators of its particular ethos rather than new starts for the twentieth-century outlook, of which the early Hemingway is probably more representative. *The Sun Also Rises* is a functional twentieth-century house, while *Ulysses* or *Remembrance of Things Past* are Victorian mansions.

On the other hand, there is no reason per se for assuming that the novel is doomed. The very special conditions upon which the epic depended and which made its existence impossible once they disappeared have no real analogy in the history of the novel. Furthermore there have been in the past, in the history of the English novel, periods of stagnation, as, for example, in the late eighteenth century, before Scott and Austen, and in the early nineteenth century, before Dickens and the great Victorians. It is possible for two such giants as Lawrence and Joyce to exhaust momentarily the possibilities of a medium, for between them both they seem to say everything that can be said. Like Scott and Austen, a century before, they seem to have divided all human experience, and then, each in his own province, to have done everything that could be done. All of the Victorians were brought up on Sir Walter, and each thought in his youth that there was to be no "competing" with *this*. But compete with him they did, and in many cases surpassed him.

Just so, Lawrence and Joyce now look overpowering, and partly because of the antithetical nature of their talents: to abjure one is to compete with the other. Joyce is the great "artificer," Lawrence the great "natural"; Joyce celebrates the mystery of fatherhood and represents the male principle, while Lawrence is the voice of womanhood and her mysteries; Joyce describes the intricacies of the city, while Lawrence is the rhapsodist of nature; Joyce examines the illogicalities of conscious and unconscious life, Lawrence the wordless ways of the instincts; Joyce is the voice of Catholicism, Lawrence of Protestantism; Joyce is the cosmopolite, Lawrence the provincial; Joyce stands for history, Lawrence for futurity; Joyce is a Rabelaisian comedian, Lawrence a Puritan prophet; Joyce apotheosizes the family, Lawrence romantic love; Joyce describes, Lawrence evokes; for Joyce sex is of the devil, for Lawrence it is a religion; Joyce portrays the pathos of frustration, Lawrence prophecies an imagined release and fulfillment; Joyce thought language an ultimate reality, Lawrence thought it an ultimate sham. Psychologically, culturally, artistically, they are antithetical in every respect, and they stand like great roadblocks whose existence seems to imperil any fresh starts.

But they are roadblocks of a differing order, Joyce a real one, Lawrence only an apparent one. *Finnegan* is a literal "wake" for a certain kind of novel, but *The Man Who Died* is an allegory pointing to a prose fiction of the future. Joyce's work carries the exploration of the psyche, literary elaboration, the sense of human frustration, and linguistic experimentation as far as they can be carried, and *Finnegans Wake* is the point of no return. But Lawrence, for all his resemblances and indebtednesses to Butler and Forster, represents a fresh start, or, better, a renewal.

Sociologically, he is a rebel against the individualism and the inhibitions of the middle class; artistically, he is the apostle of "naturalness," as opposed to "artifice"; psychologically, he is interested in instincts rather than the data of consciousness; ontologically, he stands for the idea of growth as against the idea of stasis; and, above all, he is perhaps the most striking representative of that late nineteenth and early twentieth century phenomenon: the reentry of the Bible into the main stream of European culture from which it had been excluded during most of the eighteenth century and most of the nineteenth century. All over the late nineteenth century, the Bible, supposedly permanently crippled by mid-nineteenth century science and rationalism, begins to reappear, as vigorous as ever. The major impulse behind Dostoevsky, as he himself said, was the Book of Job; for Tolstoy it was the New Testament; for Matthew Arnold the Bible as a whole; for Thomas Hardy the pessimistic parts of the Old Testament. Old Testament pessimism was likewise stamped into Melville's consciousness, and lies at the heart of *Moby Dick*.

Lawrence's interest in the Bible, however, and its force in his novels, lay in a different realm from any of these others, all of whom went to the Bible for philosophical or moral sustenance. In the first place, Lawrence did not like the climax of the Bible—the ending of the Four Gospels—and his last creative act was to rewrite Matthew, Mark, Luke, and John in *The Man Who Died*. The Bible that he loved was contained in the early books of the Old Testament, in Genesis, Exodus, Samuel, and Kings. Furthermore, it was not the didacticism of the Bible that attracted him, and he always insisted that, despite the fact that he was a "prophet," his own novels were nondidactic and simply represented life as fully and as deeply as possible.

Rather it was the *spirit* of the earlier parts of the Old Testament that attracted him and which he tried to inject into his own novels—the vigor, the fierceness, the elemental passions, and the closeness to the earth, from which the first Father and Mother had arisen in the opening chapters of Genesis. If any part of Christianity genuinely attracted him it was the militant aspect of Protestantism. In "Hymns in a Man's Life" he said that even deeper woven into his consciousness than such early literary influences as Wordsworth or Shakespeare or Keats were the banal Nonconformist hymns that dominated his childhood memories. He was proud of the fact that he was a Congregationalist, the oldest of the Nonconformist sects, because, in his childhood anyway, it had escaped the ghastly sentimentalism that had come in with Methodism and because it was vigorous and joyful.

So too it was the rapturously and rigorously physical depiction of life in the early parts of the Old Testament that fired his imagination and animated his novels, both in their content and in their style. The incantatory prose of Lawrence, at its best and at its worst, is purely Biblical, and a page of it could be put side by side with, say, "The Song of Solomon," and there would be no essential differences: there is the concreteness of everything, the short, rapt, bardic utterance, and the oracular repetitiousness. Characters likewise have their whole instinctual life motivated by Biblical imagery and utterance, particularly, generation by generation, in *The Rainbow-Women in Love* series. When Lydia and Tom Brangwen after two years of rather tense married life, finally come together in a deep sense, Lawrence describes it thus: "When at last they had joined hands, the house was finished, and the Lord took up his abode. And they were glad." And Anna, Lydia's daughter by her first marriage, at last feels confident in her parents: "She played between the pillar of fire and the pillar of cloud in confidence, having the assurance on her right hand and the assurance on her left. She was no longer called upon to uphold with her childish might the broken end of the arch. Her father and her mother now met to the span of the heavens, and she, the child, was free to play in the space beneath, between." With Anna herself, as she grows up, the Biblical sense and utterance become more pronounced, and, at times, embarrassing. When pregnant, after her marriage to Will, she takes off her clothes and dances, for, "She liked the story of David, who danced before the Lord, and uncovered himself exultingly." With Ursula, their child, the Biblical sense becomes even more emphatic. Although she hates sermons, she loves Sundays; by day she sees in a vision the white-robed spirit of Christ passing between the olive trees and by night she hears a voice calling "Samuel, Samuel!" Her favorite book is Genesis and her favorite text, which motivates her whole life, is Genesis VI, 2–4, which begins: "The Sons of God saw the daughters of men that they were fair: and they took them wives of all which they chose." This passage stirs her like a call. There must be, she thinks, offspring of God, Sons of God, other than Jesus and Adam, men who had neither given up the life of the body nor been driven ignominiously from Paradise, and who "came on free feet to the daughters of men, and took them to wife, so that the women conceived and brought forth men of renown." Her whole instinctual life then is centered on finding for a mate a "Son of God." When she first sees Skrebensky, she imagines him as "one such as those Sons of God who saw the daughters of men, that they were fair"; she soon sees that he is Adamic and fallen. But in the sequel to *The Rainbow*, in *Women in Love*, Ursula finally finds, after much turmoil and struggle, her "Son of God" in Birkin. After they finally capitulate to one another, she thinks: "This was release at last. She had had lovers, she had known passion. But this was neither love nor passion. It was the daughters of men coming back to the sons of God, the strange inhuman sons of God who are in the beginning."

For the Bible, said Lawrence, was "in my bones." [10] He thought it was "a great confused novel" and that the novel itself was "the book of life." The Bible was not about God, but about "man alive." "Adam, Eve, Sarai, Abraham, Isaac, Jacob, Samuel, David, Bathsheba, Ruth, Esther, Solomon, Job, Isaiah, Jesus, Mark, Judas, Paul, Peter: what is it but man alive, from start to finish." [11]

The "man alive" that Mayhew, with disapproval, and Butler, with approval, saw in the upper and lower classes and that Lawrence saw in his own lower class had already been prefigured in the opening pages of the earliest and greatest of Western "novels," the Bible.

The saturation in the Bible, the feeling for the natural world, the passionate surge of impulse from the "lower orders" up into the world of educated-intellectualized consciousness, the opposition of "life" to "literature" — "storytelling" to "artifice," "speech" to "style" — the anarchist-instinctual rebellion against codes and restrictions and rationality and rules are obviously not unique with Lawrence. One or more or all of these characteristics calls up memories of Langland, Bunyan, Blake, Wordsworth, George Orwell — the whole anarchist tradition in English literature, a tradition that accounts for much of the strength of the greatest of the Western literatures which, because of this tradition, is forever renewing itself in the Bible, in the instinctual life and in the plangent organisms of its native soil. This is not to say that the anarchist tradition constitutes the primary strength of English literature; on the contrary, it is the Chaucers, Shakespeares, and Miltons who are its towering geniuses. But considered as historical forces, as influences, the supreme writers are positively baneful. Shakespeare helped to ruin the English verse drama just as surely as Milton helped to kill off the English verse epic, and just as surely did Joyce finish off the "psychological" and "literary" novel. There is no emulation of a genius and, historically, he serves only to create a moribund tradition.

On the other hand, the immense creative powers and accomplishments of the anarchist tradition must not be underestimated either. Its two most fierce and greatest representatives are Blake and Lawrence, and they must be accounted in the first rank of English poets and novelists. But good or bad, the anarchists are always movers and shakers, who constantly renew and revitalize literature and open doors to the future. And their existence is a constant reminder that every Milton needs his Bunyan, every Pope his Blake and Wordsworth, every Joyce his Lawrence.

NOTES

1—Henry James: *The Poetics of Empiricism*

1. Austin Warren, *Rage for Order* (Chicago, 1948), pp. 146–61. Warren speaks of the basic ingredients of the late works, dramatic dialogue and highly metaphorical descriptions of states of consciousness, as "dialectic" and "myth," respectively.

2. Quentin Anderson, "Henry James and the New Jerusalem," *Kenyon Review*, VIII (1946), 515–66. There is neither space nor occasion for a summary of this complex essay. For the miniscule sketch of recent James criticism being given here two quotations will suffice: "Since the elder James was a theologian and a moralist, it is conceivable that he stood in the same relation to the novelist as Aquinas does to Dante or Kierkegaard to Kafka" (p. 515); "In the end James is not a tragic poet but the poet of his father's theodicy" (p. 565). Anderson's theories are further elaborated in "the Two Henry James," *Scrutiny*, XIV (1947), 242–51, and "Henry James, His Symbolism and His Critics," *Scrutiny*, XV (1947), 12–19.

3. Henry Bamford Parkes, "The James Brothers," *Sewanee Review*, LVI (1948), 323–28. Parkes says, e.g., that the use by Henry James of a scrupulously observed "point of view" rather than the customary novelistic convention of authorial omniscience was the artistic counterpart of the pragmatist theory that no truth has absolute validity and, hence, everything is relative to the observer.

4. "The meaning of his [James] works has been obscured by its subject matter . . . the deeper significance of his work is to be found not in its subject matter but in its mode of construction" (ibid., p. 326).

5. "The Great Mr. Locke: America's Philosopher,

1783–1861," *Huntington Library Bulletin,* No. 11 (April 1937), pp. 107–51.

6. "The Social Significance of Our Institutions," *American Philosophic Addresses,* ed. Joseph T. Blair (New York, 1946), p. 248.

7. The exposition of the ultimate implications of Locke's doctrines is based generally upon A. N. Whitehead's familiar thesis that Locke effected a "bifurcation of nature," which broke up any organic relationship between man and nature and man and man, and made each individual an isolated mental substance. I am indebted especially to the detailed working out of this thesis by F. S. C. Northrop, *The Meeting of East and West* (New York, 1947), pp. 80–111.

8. *The Novels and Tales of Henry James* (New York, 1907), II, 3–4. Hereafter all references to James will be given in this edition.

9. "Henry James," *Yale Review,* XIX (Spring 1930), 641.

10. *The Possessed,* trans. Constance Garnett (New York, 1913), p. 549.

11. *The Wound and the Bow* (New York, 1947), p. 99.

12. *Henry James at Work* (London, 1924), p. 33.

13. *Philosophy in a New Key* (New York, 1948), pp. 1–2.

2—Mann's Double Vision: Doctor Faustus *and* The Holy Sinner

1. The passages quoted from *Doctor Faustus,* copyright 1948, by Alfred A. Knopf, Inc., and *The Holy Sinner,* copyright 1951, by Alfred A. Knopf, Inc., are herewith reprinted with the kind permission of the publisher.

4—Fitzgerald's The Great Gatsby: *Legendary Bases and Allegorical Significances*

1. It should be added that there is one more mention of the far West and this time in a joke (Fitzgerald's). When Gatsby is telling Nick the preposterous dream story of his imaginary career, Nick asks him, casually, what part of the "Middle West" he comes from, and Gatsby replies "San Francisco."

6—What Scott Meant to the Victorians

1. C. M. Grieve, *Albyn* (London, 1927), p. 86.
2. Macdiarmid, *Lucky Poet* (London, 1943), p. 202.

3. *The Letters of John Keats,* ed. Hyder Rollins (Cambridge, 1958), II, 16.

4. *The Critical Opinions of William Wordsworth,* ed. Markham Peacock (Baltimore, 1950), p. 340.

5. See James Hillhouse, *The Waverley Novels and their Critics* (London, 1936).

6. *Letters of Samuel Taylor Coleridge,* ed. Earl Leslie Griggs (Oxford, 1959), III, 360–61.

7. *The Journal of Eugène Delacroix,* ed. Hubert Wellington (London, 1951), p. 205.

8. James L. Caw, *Scottish Painting* (Edinburgh, n.d.), pp. 94, 97, 108, 147–49, 477, and *passim.*

9. A. J. Finberg, *The Life of J. M. W. Turner* (Oxford, 1961), pp. 332–33, 334.

10. *Life of Sir Walter Scott* (London, 1900), I, 394.

11. Henry-Russell Hitchcock, *Early Victorian Architecture in Britain* (New Haven, 1954), pp. 245–48.

12. *Essays on Fiction* (London, 1864). Senior's reviews were originally published in the *Quarterly, Edinburgh, London,* and *North British* Reviews. In reviewing the earlier Waverleys Senior was unaware that Scott was the author. For example, in reviewing *Ivanhoe* he picked up a heraldic error and noted its coincidence with "a similar mistake in his great rival, Sir Walter Scott": "The Black Knight bears what Rebecca calls a 'bar and padlock painted blue,' or, as Ivanhoe corrects her, 'a fetterlock and shackle bolt azure' on a black shield; that is, azure upon sable. This, as colour upon colour, is false heraldry. Now on the shield of Sir Walter's Marmion, a falcon 'Soared sable in an azure field.' The same fault reversed. It is a curious addition to the coincidences of these two great writers, that, with all their minute learning on chivalrous points, they should both have been guilty of the same oversight" (pp. 52–53). In reviewing *The Fortunes of Nigel* Senior noted the archetypal Waverley situation—a virtuous and passive hero who marries the heroine; a fierce, active hero who dies a violent death; and a fool or bore (Caleb in *Lammermoor* or Dalgetty in *Montrose*)—and said, "it is too obvious an imitation of Sir Walter Scott" (p. 101).

13. The analogy to a feast is not fanciful: "Today [8 Oct. 1820] I perform alone upon a roast chicken, and mean to devour 'Kenilworth' with it. There are different opinions. Charles Greville told me last night that he did not stir out

or go to bed till five in the morning the day he begun it"; see *Letters of Harriet Countess Granville, 1810–1845,* ed F. L. Gower (London, 1894), I, 186.

14. *Life of Scott,* III, 209–11. These judicial and part by part assessments of Scott's novels occur frequently in Victorian letters, biographies, and memoirs. For example, in a letter to Lord Abercorn of 18 Jan. 1818, the Earl of Aberdeen discussed *Rob Roy,* which was good on five points (characters and scenes) but bad on five others (characters and plot); each work of the unknown author had its characteristic "excellence": see Lady Frances Balfour, *The Life of George Fourth Earl of Aberdeen* (London, 1922), I, 198–99. In Sydney Colvin's *Memories and Notes of Persons and Places* (New York, 1921), pp. 196–98, there is recounted a detailed and authoritative structural analysis of *The Bride of Lammermoor* that might give pause to a New Critic—given by Mr. Gladstone.

15. "Wordsworth's Fame," in *All in Due Time* (London, 1955), p. 43.

16. *The Notebooks of Henry James,* ed. F. O. Matthiessen and Kenneth Murdock (New York, 1947), p. 36.

17. Ernest Hartley Coleridge, *Life and Correspondence of John Duke Lord Coleridge* (London, 1904), p. 359.

18. Frederic Maitland, *Life and Letters of Leslie Stephen* (London, 1906), p. 458.

19. Harriet Martineau, *Miscellanies* (Boston, 1836), I, 48–49.

20. Rowland E. Prothero, *The Life and Correspondence of Dean Stanley* (London, 1893), p. 384.

21. *The Works and Life of Walter Bagehot,* ed. Mrs. Russell Barrington (London, 1915), III, 37–72.

22. Duke of Argyll, *Autobiography and Memories* (London, 1906), II, 196.

23. Victorians seemed at times to like Scott even for his defects: Countess Granville wrote, "I delight in even the faults of the novels, 'Ivanhoe' excepted." (*Letters,* I, 181).

24. G B-J, *Memorials of Edward Burne-Jones* (London, 1904), II, 329.

25. Macaulay and his sister once made the *Mysteries of Udolpho* the prize of a bet between them as to who could make the most puns in conversation over a certain period of time (Macaulay won with two-hundred bad puns in two

hours); see G. O. Trevelyan, *The Life and Letters of Lord Macaulay* (New York, 1876), I, 170.

26. *Sir Robert Peel*, ed. Charles S. Parker (London, 1899), I, 319.

27. *Collected Essays* (London, 1925), I, 190.

28. H. J. C. Grierson, "Scott and Carlyle," in *Essays and Studies* (London, 1928), XIII, 88, 90.

29. *The George Eliot Letters*, ed. Gordon Haight (New Haven, 1954–55), V, 174–75.

30. *The Journal of Sir Walter Scott*, ed. J. G. Tait (Edinburgh, 1950), p. 53.

31. *The Life of Napoleon Buonaparte* (Exeter, 1836), I, 33.

32. *The Westminster Review*, VIII (1828), 296.

33. Scott as a conscious philosopher of history was old-style even in his own day when the great secular philosophies of history were beginning to arise. In his Introduction, originally written in 1887, to Scott's *The Tales of a Grandfather* (London, 1911), F. W. Farrar said Scott "would have said with the great Vico, that 'History is a civil theology of Divine Providence'; with Bolingbroke that it is 'Philosophy teaching by examples'; with Wilhelm von Humboldt, that 'The History of the world is not intelligible apart from a government of the world'; and with Fichte, that 'Every step in advance in history is an inflowing of God'; 'God alone makes history, but he does this by the agency of man' " (p. xv). Farrar notes that since *Tales of a Grandfather* was written there had been conceived at least fourteen French and thirteen German philosophies of history, all of them tending "to become more technical, more elaborate, more exhaustive and more scientific" (p. xix). Scott then represented the "power of bright narration." If Scott himself in *Tales of a Grandfather* points any historical moral, it is that good comes out of evil although, "We must not do evil even that good may come of it" (p. 47).

34. *Letters of Sir Walter Scott*, ed. H. J. C. Grierson (London, 1932), XI, 455.

35. *British Novelists and their Styles* (London, 1859), p. 176.

36. Leslie Stephen, "Sir Walter Scott," *Hours in a Library* (London, 1907), I, 186–229. The essay on Scott was originally published in 1871.

37. *Coleridge's Miscellaneous Criticism*, ed. T. M. Raysor (London, 1936), pp. 341–42.

38. Sir Lewis Namier makes somewhat the same point about the logic of irrational traditions when discussing secret service pensions in the time of George III: "they show . . . the charitable character of that very humane institution, and the utter unimportance of the acquisitions which the Government made through it"; see *The Structure of Politics at the Accession of George III*, 2nd ed. (London, 1957), p. xii.

39. In his *History of Scotland* (Philadelphia, 1830), Scott concludes his account of the accession of James I by saying the disadvantages of the union of the crowns, which marked the beginning of the end for Scotland as an indigenous culture, were "finally incalculably overbalanced by the subsequent benefits" (p. 427). But previous to this he quotes a long lament made by an old man to James before he left for London about Scotland becoming England's province. Some of the impossibilities involved in a Scotsman committing himself on either side of this momentous question of the Union can be glimpsed from a statement by Macdiarmid: "I believe that the Industrial Revolution would have spread to Scotland much less injuriously if England had suddenly disappeared about 1700" (*Albyn*, p. 29).

40. *Posthistoric Man* (Chapel Hill, N. C., 1950), pp. 337–38.

41. Quoted by Mark Schorer, *Sinclair Lewis* (New York, 1961), p. 331.

7—Dickens and the Sense of Time

1. Humphrey House, *The Dickens World* (Oxford, 1942); Kathleen Tillotson, *Novels of the Eighteen-Forties* (Oxford, 1954).

2. Andrew Lang (ed.), *The Works of Charles Dickens* (London, 1897), VIII, 1. All references will be given in this, the Gadshill edition.

3. Writing to Forster of the plot of *Little Dorrit* Dickens said, "It struck me that it would be a new thing to show people coming together, in a chance way, as fellow-travelers, and being in the same place, ignorant of one another, as happens in life; and to connect them afterwards, and to make the waiting for that connection a part of the interest." (*The Letters of Charles Dickens* [Bloomsbury, 1938], II, 685).

4. Stephen Leacock remarks, "Incidentally one notices how fond Dickens was of these 'forward references,' the insertion of such items of assertion or reflection, only to be understood later" (*Charles Dickens* [New York, 1936], p. 57). But Monroe Engel points out that he objected to overanticipating or to giving the reader too many hints ("Dickens on Art," *Modern Philology*, LIII [August, 1955], 35).

5. Even the high priest of "the point of view," Percy Lubbock, allowed *David Copperfield* in the inner sanctuary of the blest and he speaks approvingly of "the large rhythm of Copperfield's memory" (*The Craft of Fiction* [London, 1921], p. 129). George Ford points out that a contemporary reviewer recognized this merit in the novel and remarked upon it (*Dickens and His Readers* [Princeton, 1955], p. 128). Generations of readers can only agree.

8—Victorian Morals and the Modern Novel

1. Henry Mayhew, *London Labour and the London Poor* (London, 1861), I, 43.

2. *The Letters of Charles Dickens* [Bloomsbury, 1939], II, 767.

3. See Kathleen Tillotson's excellent *Novels of the Eighteen-Forties* (Oxford, 1954), pp. 54–58.

4. D. H. Lawrence, *The Letters of . . .* , ed. by Aldous Huxley (New York, 1932), p. 441.

5. D. H. Lawrence, *Phoenix* (New York, 1936), p. 410.

6. "E.T." *D. H. Lawrence* (London, 1935), p. 105.

7. *Ibid.*, p. 105.

8. *The Later D. H. Lawrence*, ed. by W. Y. Tindall (New York, 1952), p. 192.

9. D. H. Lawrence, *Selected Literary Criticism* (New York, 1956), p. 5.

10. *Ibid.*, p. 164.

11. *Ibid.*, p .105.

INDEX

Albert, Prince, 139, 144
Allan, William, 103
Aquinas, Thomas, 3
Arendt, Hannah, 123
Aristotle, 15, 78
Arnold, Matthew, 143, 149, 160
Asbury, Francis, 80
Augustine, Saint, 92
Austen, Jane, x, 100, 101, 159

Bagehot, Walter, 98, 109–10, 118, 119–20, 120–21
Balfour, Lady Francis, 167
Beardsley, Aubrey, 181
Beecher, Henry Ward, 111
Beethoven, Ludwig von, 33, 40, 41
Berdyaev, Nicholas: and the three kinds of time, 45–46; 51, 53
Bergson, Henri, 45
Bible, The: in *The Damnation of Theron Ware*, 82–83, 91–92; re-entry into Western literature in nineteenth century, 160
Blake, William, 74, 163
Bosanquet, Theodora, 22
Brontës, The: as writers, 117;

Wurthering Heights and *Jane Eyre*, 141
Brooks, Van Wyck, *The Wine of the Puritans*, 71, 71–72, 74
Bunyan, John, 163
Burke, Edmond, 116, 120
Burne-Jones, Sir Edward, 111
Burns, Robert, 97
Butler, Bishop, 73
Butler, Samuel: attack on Victorian morality, 150; *The Way of All Flesh*, 142, 149, 152, 154, 155, 156, 157, 159–60, 163
Byron, Lord, 98, 100

Cadell, Robert, 103
Carlyle, Thomas, *The French Revolution*, 98, 110, 113, 116
Cervantes, Miguel, *Don Quixote*, 43, 55, 101, 118
Chaucer, Geoffrey, 163
Chopin, Frederick, 76, 82
Cockburn, Lord, 122
Cohen, Morris, x
Coleridge, Lord, 107–8
Coleridge, Samuel Taylor, 99, 100, 116, 117, 120, 121, 122, 123

In the many writers discussed herein John Henry Raleigh sees the growth of the novel to its present preeminence. **Sir Walter Scott's** descriptions of Scotch history and scenery and **Charles Dickens'** unforgettable characters helped popularize the form. In rebellion against the Victorians **Samuel Butler** satirized hypocrisy and convention in *The Way of All Flesh*; **E. M. Forster** studied emotional conflicts between individuals in *The Longest Journey* and *A Passage to India*; **D. H. Lawrence** used symbolism in *Lady Chatterley's Lover* and *Women in Love*. The Americans were not far behind, as **Harold Frederic** offered convincing descriptions of social problems in *The Damnation of Theron Ware*; **Henry James** pioneered a psychological realism in *A Portrait of a Lady* and *The Ambassadors*; **F. Scott Fitzgerald's** *The Great Gatsby* compellingly described the human condition. The German author **Thomas Mann** brought to the novel a mythological psychology in his "Joseph" series, and Mr. Raleigh argues that *The Holy Sinner* is a coda of the series.